GLEIM® | Aviation

SEVENTH EDITION

INSTRUMENT PILOT
Syllabus

by

Irvin N. Gleim, Ph.D., CFII

and

Garrett W. Gleim, CFII

ABOUT THE AUTHORS

Irvin N. Gleim earned his private pilot certificate in 1965 from the Institute of Aviation at the University of Illinois, where he subsequently received his Ph.D. He is a commercial pilot and flight instructor (instrument) with multi-engine and seaplane ratings and is a member of the Aircraft Owners and Pilots Association, American Bonanza Society, Civil Air Patrol, Experimental Aircraft Association, National Association of Flight Instructors, and Seaplane Pilots Association. He is the author of flight maneuvers and practical test prep books for the sport, private, instrument, commercial, and flight instructor certificates/ratings and the author of study guides for the remote, sport, private/recreational, instrument, commercial, flight/ground instructor, fundamentals of instructing, airline transport pilot, and flight engineer FAA knowledge tests. Three additional pilot training books are *Pilot Handbook*, *Aviation Weather and Weather Services*, and *FAR/AIM*.

Dr. Gleim has also written articles for professional accounting and business law journals and is the author of widely used review manuals for the CIA (Certified Internal Auditor) exam, the CMA (Certified Management Accountant) exam, the CPA (Certified Public Accountant) exam, and the EA (IRS Enrolled Agent) exam. He is Professor Emeritus, Fisher School of Accounting, University of Florida, and is a CFM, CIA, CMA, and CPA.

Garrett W. Gleim earned his private pilot certificate in 1997 in a Piper Super Cub. He is a commercial pilot (single- and multi-engine), ground instructor (advanced and instrument), and flight instructor (instrument and multi-engine), and he is a member of the Aircraft Owners and Pilots Association, the National Association of Flight Instructors, and the Society of Aviation and Flight Educators. He is the author of study guides for the remote, sport, private/recreational, instrument, commercial, flight/ground instructor, fundamentals of instructing, and airline transport pilot FAA knowledge tests. He received a Bachelor of Science in Economics from The Wharton School, University of Pennsylvania. Mr. Gleim is also a CPA.

Gleim Publications, Inc.
PO Box 12848
Gainesville, Florida 32604

(352) 375-0772
(800) 87-GLEIM or (800) 874-5346

www.GleimAviation.com
aviationteam@gleim.com

For updates to the first printing of the seventh edition of
Instrument Pilot Syllabus

Go To: www.GleimAviation.com/updates

Or: Email update@gleim.com with **IPSYL 7-1** in the subject line. You will receive our current update as a reply.

Updates are available until the next edition is published.

ISSN 1527-0920
ISBN 978-1-61854-426-1

Let Us Know!

This syllabus is designed specifically for private pilots who aspire to obtain the instrument rating.

Please submit any corrections and suggestions for subsequent editions to the authors at www.GleimAviation.com/Questions.

Also, please bring Gleim books to the attention of flight instructors, fixed-base operators, and others interested in flying. Wide distribution of this series of books and increased interest in flying depend on your assistance and good word. Thank you.

Environmental Statement -- This book is printed on recycled paper sourced from suppliers certified using sustainable forestry management processes.

If necessary, we will develop an UPDATE for *Instrument Pilot Syllabus*. Visit our website or email update@gleim.com for the latest updates. Updates for this edition will be available until the next edition is published. To continue providing our customers with first-rate service, we request that technical questions about our materials be sent to us via www.GleimAviation.com/Questions. We will give each question thorough consideration and a prompt response. Questions concerning orders, prices, shipments, or payments will be handled via telephone by our competent and courteous customer service staff.

TABLE OF CONTENTS

IF FOUND, PLEASE CONTACT

Pilot Name _____

Address _____

_____

_____

Telephone # _____

Email _____

PREFACE

Thank you for choosing Gleim. Our training materials (books, software, audios, and online) are intuitively appealing and thus very effective in transferring knowledge to you. The Gleim system saves you time, money, and frustration vs. other aviation training programs.

This syllabus will facilitate your studies and training for your instrument rating.

1. Please read the following Introduction carefully.

2. The "Lesson Sequence and Times" section shows ground lessons being completed as you complete flight lessons. We encourage you to work ahead in your ground lessons and begin them (and even complete them) prior to beginning your flight training.

3. The **objective** is to develop "ACS level" proficiency as quickly as possible. "ACS level" means you can perform at the level required by the FAA's Airman Certification Standards.

4. Homework consists of reading and/or studying your Gleim reference books or online courseware and the Pilot's Operating Handbook or Operating Limitations for your airplane. Each flight lesson also directs you to review topics and material studied for previous lessons.

   a. The Instrument Pilot Kit does not contain **Pilot Handbook** or **FAR/AIM** since these books are included in the Gleim Private Pilot Kit. If you do not have them, please order your copies today.

Why is the GLEIM SYSTEM different? It focuses on successful completion, as quickly and as easily as possible. The requirements for earning your instrument rating are listed beginning on page 2. This syllabus facilitates your flight training so you achieve an "ACS level" of proficiency on the 20 required FAA "tasks" as quickly as possible for airplane single-engine land!

GO FOR IT! Start studying for your FAA instrument rating knowledge test today. Refer to **Instrument Pilot FAA Knowledge Test Prep** and associated textbooks. Start studying for your FAA practical test by reading Study Unit 3 of **Instrument Pilot Flight Maneuvers and Practical Test Prep**.

We have an easy-to-follow and easy-to-complete study system. From the very start, we want you to focus on success. This means answering over 80% of the FAA knowledge test questions correctly AND being able to explain and demonstrate the 20 required FAA practical test tasks to your CFII at "ACS level" proficiency for airplane single-engine land.

Enjoy Flying Safely!

Irvin N. Gleim
Garrett W. Gleim

December 2020

INTRODUCTION

This syllabus is a step-by-step lesson plan for your instrument rating training. It is intended to be used in conjunction with the current edition of the following six Gleim books:

Instrument Pilot FAA Knowledge Test Prep
Instrument Pilot Flight Maneuvers and Practical Test Prep
Instrument Pilot ACS and Oral Exam Guide
Aviation Weather and Weather Services
Pilot Handbook
FAR/AIM

Your flight instructor (or flight school) will retain a copy of each flight lesson page in this book (and/or make use of the Gleim Instrument Pilot Training Record) as you complete the flight lesson. If a copier is not available at the conclusion of your flight lesson, bring a copy of the completed flight lesson page to the next flight lesson.

WHAT ELSE DO YOU NEED?

If you purchased this syllabus as part of the Gleim **Instrument Pilot Kit**, you will need IFR low en route and instrument approach charts. Sources for charts include

1. **Aeronautical Information Services.** The FAA's Aeronautical Information Services is the aeronautical charting authority for the development, publication, and dissemination of aeronautical charts. Printed FAA IFR charts may be purchased through online vendors as well as some fixed-base operators (FBO) at a local airport.

2. **Jeppesen Sanderson, Inc. (JEPP)**, is a private competitor to the FAA's chart publications. It is the most widely used chart service, and the graphic presentation of its charts differs from that of FAA charts in a number of respects. However, the information is furnished by the FAA.

Appendix C, "IFR Aeronautical Charts," in the **Instrument Pilot Flight Maneuvers and Practical Test Prep** book has more information on the basic IFR charts and how to order the charts.

Additionally, you will need to purchase a copy of the Pilot's Operating Handbook (POH) (sometimes called an Information Manual) for the make and model of your training airplane. Alternatively, you may make a photocopy if the POH is not available for purchase.

REQUIREMENTS FOR AN INSTRUMENT RATING

You must meet a number of requirements to earn your instrument rating. The final step is your FAA practical test, which will be conducted by an appropriate evaluator. Your practical test will consist of an approximately 1- to 2-hour oral exam followed by a 1- to 2-hour flight test. You will be well prepared for your practical test by your CFII and your Gleim pilot training materials. In addition, you must meet the following requirements:

1. Hold at least a private pilot certificate with an airplane category rating and single-engine class rating.

    a. Part 61 students must have logged 50 hours of cross-country pilot-in-command time. This is not required of Part 141 students.

2. Be able to read, write, and converse fluently in English (certificates with operating limitations may be available for medically related deficiencies).

3. Hold a current FAA medical certificate or operate under BasicMed.

    a. Your medical exam will be conducted by an FAA-designated aviation medical examiner (AME).

    b. Ask your CFII or call your local flight school for the names and telephone numbers of the AMEs in your area, or visit www.faa.gov/pilots/amelocator for a listing of AMEs by state and city.

    c. Use the FAA MedXPress system to create an account and complete the initial portion of the application before you meet with your AME.

        1) Access the system at http://medxpress.faa.gov.

    d. BasicMed allows a pilot to conduct certain VFR and IFR operations using a U.S. driver's license instead of a medical certificate as long as the pilot meets the conditions found in 14 CFR 61.23 and 14 CFR Part 68.

4. Pass your FAA instrument rating airman knowledge test, which consists of 60 multiple-choice questions administered at an FAA-designated computer testing center. Everything you need to prepare for your FAA instrument rating (airplane) airman knowledge test is in your Gleim *Instrument Pilot FAA Knowledge Test Prep, Instrument Pilot Flight Maneuvers and Practical Test Prep, FAR/AIM, Pilot Handbook,* and *Aviation Weather and Weather Services* books. The Gleim **FAA Test Prep Online** will facilitate your study. Use the Gleim **Online Ground School** for convenient, complete knowledge test study from any computer with Internet access.

    a. We have estimated 30 hours to completely prepare for your instrument rating airman knowledge test. "Instrument Rating Syllabus Lesson Sequence and Times," beginning on page 10, has more information.

    b. The further you study for your FAA instrument rating airman knowledge test before you commence your flight lessons, the better!

        1) Under Part 141, you should be enrolled in the school's instrument rating course before beginning your study program.

5. Undertake flight training as described in Lessons 1 through 29. Many of the lessons may require more than one flight to complete. We also have provided space for your instructor to record extra flights within each lesson as needed to make you comfortable and proficient.

    a. It's fun to be successful! Be overly prepared before you get to the airport for each flight lesson.

 The KEY TO SUCCESS in your flight training, which also minimizes cost and frustration, is your study and preparation at home before flying with your flight instructor. The more you know about flying, flight training, and each flight lesson, the better you will do.

6. PASS your FAA practical test. See Study Unit 3 (in Part I) in *Instrument Pilot Flight Maneuvers and Practical Test Prep*.

For additional detail regarding FAA instrument rating requirements, refer to the Introduction in the *Instrument Pilot FAA Knowledge Test Prep* book or pages 2 and 3 in the *Instrument Pilot Flight Maneuvers and Practical Test Prep* book.

HOW TO PROCEED

1. We recommend obtaining a Gleim **Deluxe Instrument Pilot Kit** from your FBO/flight school/bookstore. For publisher-direct service, visit www.GleimAviation.com or call (800) 874-5346.

    The **Deluxe Instrument Pilot Kit** contains **Online Ground School**, **FAA Test Prep Online**, **Audio Review** (optional download), plus study and reference books, including *Instrument Pilot FAA Knowledge Test Prep*, *Instrument Pilot Flight Maneuvers and Practical Test Prep*, *Instrument Pilot ACS and Oral Exam Guide*, *Aviation Weather and Weather Services*, a **Training Record**, and this *Instrument Pilot Syllabus*.

2. Read this Introduction (13 pages).

3. Obtain a current and valid medical certificate (if necessary).

4. Begin preparing for your FAA instrument rating airman knowledge test by using your Gleim books, **FAA Test Prep Online**, and/or **Online Ground School**. See your ground training syllabus.

5. Select a CFII and/or flight school. Study Unit 1 in *Instrument Pilot Flight Maneuvers and Practical Test Prep* has suggestions on how to proceed.

6. Begin your flight training, scheduling at least two lessons a week. Prepare thoroughly at home for each flight lesson. Use the flight training syllabus in this book.

PART 141 VS. PART 61 SCHOOLS

Title 14 of the Code of Federal Regulations (14 CFR) lists the requirements to obtain your instrument rating. Pilot (or flight) schools can conduct your training by following either 14 CFR Part 141 or 14 CFR Part 61.

An eligible pilot school may be issued a Part 141 pilot school certificate by the FAA after completion of an application process. Part 141 pilot schools are more regulated than Part 61 pilot schools. Additionally, a Part 141 pilot school is required to have its facilities and airplanes inspected and the ground and flight training syllabi approved by the FAA.

The majority of pilot schools, and flight instructors not associated with a Part 141 pilot school, provide the required training specified under Part 61. Part 61 pilot schools do not require FAA approval. Part 61 requires 40 hours instrument time and 50 hours of cross-country flight time as pilot in command (PIC).

The major difference between a Part 141 and a Part 61 pilot school is that Part 141 requires an FAA approval and 35 hours of instrument time. Part 141 does not have a minimum cross-country experience requirement.

The Gleim syllabus has been reviewed by the FAA in Washington, D.C., and was found to meet the requirements of a syllabus under Part 141 or Part 61, as appropriate. However, final approval of a syllabus for use under Part 141 must come from the responsible Flight Standards office. Thus, the Gleim *Instrument Pilot Syllabus* can be used by any Part 141 school with minimum effort.

If a Part 141 pilot school cannot or will not use this syllabus, consider finding another Part 141 or Part 61 school for your training, OR please call (800) 874-5346 if you have questions or problems.

PART 141 STUDENT INFORMATION

Enrollment Prerequisites

You must hold at least a private pilot certificate, with an airplane category and single-engine land class, prior to enrolling in the flight portion of the instrument rating course. Have your CFI make a photocopy of the enrollment certificate on page 115 of this syllabus and complete it during your first lesson.

Graduation Requirements

You must complete the training specified in this syllabus, with a minimum of 30 hours of ground training in the specified aeronautical knowledge areas and a minimum of 35 hours of flight training. These requirements are reflected in the Gleim ground and flight training syllabus. At the completion of your training, your CFI should photocopy and complete the graduation certificate on page 117 of this syllabus.

Stage Checks

You must score a minimum of 80% on the knowledge test at the completion of each stage in the ground training syllabus and on the comprehensive end-of-course knowledge test at the conclusion of the ground training.

You must satisfactorily complete a stage check at the completion of each stage of the flight training syllabus, as well as a comprehensive end-of-course check when all flight training is complete.

Credit for Previous Training

You may be given credit toward this instrument rating course for previous pilot experience and knowledge [14 CFR 141.77(c)]:

1. If the credit is based on a Part 141 training course, the credit may be 50% of the requirements for this course.

2. If the credit is based on a Part 61 course, the credit cannot exceed 25% of the requirements for this course.

The receiving school will determine the amount of course credit to be given, based on a proficiency test, a knowledge test, or both.

GLEIM INSTRUMENT PILOT SYLLABUS

This syllabus consists of a ground training syllabus and a flight training syllabus. The ground and flight training may be done together as an integrated course of instruction, or each may be done separately. If done separately, the ground syllabus may be conducted as a home-study course or as a formal ground school.

This syllabus was constructed using the building-block progression of learning, in which the student is required to perform each simple task correctly before a more complex task is introduced. This method will promote the formation of correct habit patterns from the beginning.

Ground Training Syllabus

The ground training syllabus contains 11 lessons, which are divided into three stages. The ground training syllabus meets the training requirements of Appendix C to Part 141 and 14 CFR 61.65(b). The ground training can be conducted concurrently with the flight training, with the ground lessons completed in the order as outlined in the lesson matrix. Ground training may also be conducted as part of a formal ground school or as a home-study program.

It is recommended that the lessons be completed in sequence, but the syllabus is flexible enough to meet the needs of an individual student or of a particular training environment. When departing from the sequence, the instructor is responsible for considering the blocks of learning affected and, if used by a Part 141 pilot school, whether it would affect FAA approval.

Each ground lesson involves studying the appropriate section in the Gleim *Instrument Pilot Flight Maneuvers and Practical Test Prep*, *Aviation Weather and Weather Services*, *FAR/AIM*, and *Pilot Handbook*. After each study assignment is completed, you need to answer the questions in the appropriate study unit in the Gleim *Instrument Pilot FAA Knowledge Test Prep* book and review incorrect responses with your instructor.

Alternatively, the Gleim **FAA Test Prep Online** can be used to answer the questions at the end of each ground lesson. Our software contains the FAA figures and outlines in addition to the questions.

FAA Test Prep Online allows you to select either STUDY MODE or TEST MODE. In STUDY MODE, the software provides you with an immediate explanation of each answer you choose (correct or incorrect). You design each study lesson by choosing the conditions. In TEST MODE, the software can emulate the operation of the FAA-approved computer testing centers. Thus, you will have a complete understanding of exactly how to take an FAA instrument rating airman knowledge test before you go to a computer testing center. When you finish your test, you can study the questions missed and access answer explanations.

A third option for ground study is the Gleim **Online Ground School (OGS)**. OGS uses a similar approach to a traditional ground school in that each lesson is presented in order and divided into stages, per the syllabus book. The course contains audiovisual presentations, detailed study material, and quizzes for maximum retention of the information covered.

Because OGS is a self-study program delivered via the Internet, the classroom is always open, so you can study as it fits in to your schedule. When you complete the program and pass the end-of-course knowledge test, an endorsement will be provided to you that will enable you to take the FAA knowledge test at a testing center. This feature makes OGS especially valuable to those users electing to complete their ground training before beginning flight training.

At the end of each stage, you are required to complete the stage knowledge test before proceeding to the next stage. The end-of-course knowledge test is completed after the stage three knowledge test. Shortly after the end-of-course test, you should take the FAA instrument rating airman knowledge test. The stage knowledge tests in the ground syllabus will refer you to FAA figures found after the end-of-course knowledge test in this syllabus.

If this ground training is used as home study, we recommend that you complete the ground syllabus as quickly as possible and pass the FAA instrument rating airman knowledge test so you will have more time to prepare for your flight lessons.

Flight Training Syllabus

The Part 141 flight training syllabus contains 29 lessons, which are divided into three stages. It is recommended that each lesson be completed in sequential order.

Stage one of the flight training syllabus is designed to provide you with a foundation of attitude instrument flying skills.

Stage two is designed to provide you with the knowledge and skills required for holding procedures and instrument approach procedures.

Stage three is designed to provide you with practical experience in IFR cross-country flights and preparation for the FAA instrument rating practical test.

Stage checks. Stage checks are designed to ensure that you have acquired the necessary knowledge and skill. The stage one check (Lesson 13) is to ensure that you are proficient in attitude instrument flying. The stage two check (Lesson 23) is to ensure that you are proficient in holding procedures and instrument approach procedures. The stage three check (Lesson 28) is to ensure you are proficient in IFR cross-country flights. The end-of-course test (Lesson 29) is to ensure you are proficient in all instrument knowledge, risk assessment, and skill areas and are ready for the instrument rating practical test. It is also the final evaluation for a Part 141 graduation certificate.

The chief instructor (for the Part 141 training course) is responsible for ensuring that each pilot accomplishes the required stage checks and the end-of-course test. The chief instructor may delegate authority for conducting stage checks and the end-of-course test to an assistant chief instructor or a check instructor.

Stage checks will be used as a review by instructors conducting training under Part 61 to ensure that you have the appropriate knowledge and skills.

Sequence of a flight lesson. Each flight lesson will begin with a preflight briefing. During this time, your instructor should first answer any questions you may have from the previous lesson. Next, your instructor will brief you on the lesson content, followed by an evaluation of your preparation for the lesson.

During the flight portion of the lesson, your instructor should begin with those maneuvers listed as "review items" before introducing new maneuvers. The time required for each lesson will vary depending on the airport and the location of the training areas.

At the end of each lesson, your instructor will conduct a postflight critique and a preview of the next lesson. This time should be used to review the good points during the lesson, to identify and explain fully any problem areas, and to discuss how to correct the problems. In addition, it is a time for you to ask any questions you have about the flight.

The length of the preflight briefing and postflight critique will vary with each pilot and with his or her degree of preparedness for the lesson.

Repeating lessons. A flight lesson in this syllabus is considered complete when all review and/or new lesson items have met the completion standards for the lesson. If some items do not meet the standards or are simply not covered, those items must be completed to the applicable standards before the lesson is considered complete and before the student can move on to the next flight lesson.

You will notice multiple checkboxes beside lesson items in the syllabus book and even more in the training record to allow for multiple lesson attempts. It should not be assumed that a student's instrument training will take only 29 flight lessons simply because that is the number of lessons in the syllabus. It is likely and planned for that students will occasionally need to repeat lessons or certain items from lessons during this course of training.

Pilot preparation. The key to minimizing frustration and costs is preparation. You should budget an average of 2 to 4 hours of home study prior to each flight lesson. Learning will be easier when you are fully prepared so that your instructor can maximize the time spent in flight training.

USE OF A FLIGHT SIMULATION TRAINING DEVICE (FSTD) OR AN AVIATION TRAINING DEVICE (ATD)

While the Gleim *Instrument Pilot Syllabus* was designed to be used in a course of training using only an airplane, it may also be used in a course of training in which the use of a qualified and approved FSTD or ATD has been appropriately integrated with the approval of the responsible Flight Standards office. FSTDs include full flight simulators (FFSs) and flight training devices (FTDs). Aviation training devices (ATDs) include basic (BATD) and advanced (AATD) training devices.

The requirements for using an FFS or FTD in a Part 141 FAA-approved pilot training course are discussed in 14 CFR 141.41(a). FFSs and FTDs are evaluated and qualified under 14 CFR Part 60 and require annual renewal. The requirements for using an ATD are discussed in 14 CFR 141.41(b). The approval and use of an ATD is prescribed in AC 61-136. ATDs must be accompanied by the FAA letter of authorization (LOA) and are valid for 60 calendar months.

An FSTD or ATD may only be used in accordance with the authorization for each specific device. Generally, an ATD may not be used for credit toward the following types of aeronautical experience: cross-country, night, solo, lessons requiring specific quantities of takeoffs and landings, or to meet the requirement to have 3 hours of instruction within 2 calendar months of a practical test.

All training time in an FSTD/ATD must be provided by an authorized flight instructor and documented in accordance with 14 CFR 61.51. There are no restrictions on the amount of training time that may be accomplished and logged in an FSTD/ATD; however, there are regulatory limitations on the maximum credit allowed in an FFS, FTD, or ATD toward the "minimum" pilot experience requirements. Training under Part 141 in an FSTD/ATD may be credited up to the maximum time in the table below toward the 35-hour training time requirement for an instrument rating.

Device	Allowance	Hours
FFS (Part 141)	50%	17.50
FTD (Part 141)	40%	14.00
AATD (Part 141)	40%	14.00
BATD (Part 141)	25%	8.75

The specific lessons that can be accomplished in an FFS, FTD, and/or ATD are indicated with the words "FSTD/ATD option" under the lesson title. If an FSTD/ATD is available, the instructor and student should work together to determine which lessons would provide the greatest benefits while still meeting FAA requirements.

A pilot school operating under Part 61 may also elect to use an FFS, FTD, or ATD in accordance with the specific authorization for that use as outlined in the various sections of Part 61 [such as a maximum of 20 hours of flight training under 14 CFR 61.65(i)]. Time with an instructor in a BATD and an AATD may be credited toward the aeronautical experience requirements for the instrument rating as specified in the LOA for the device used. For more information, refer to the Instrument Rating Airman Certification Standards, Appendix 8, "Use of Flight Simulation Training Devices (FSTD) and Aviation Training Devices (ATD)."

AIRPLANE AND LOCAL AIRPORT(S) WORKSHEETS

During your instrument training, your CFII will provide you with the appropriate aircraft power settings and configurations to produce the desired performance. Applying this information is called "flying by the numbers" or the PAC (power setting, altitude, and configuration) method. Use the airplane worksheet to fill out the power and configuration to obtain a desired performance (e.g., 100 kt., VSI ± 500 fpm) for all phases of instrument flight. The local airport(s) worksheet is to be used as a study reference of radio frequencies, runway lengths, and types of approach(es) available at your primary airport and any other local airports you may use during your training.

AIRPLANE WORKSHEET

Phase of Flight	Power (MP/RPM)	Configuration	Performance
Initial Climb			
Cruise Climb			
Cruise			
En Route Descent			
Holding			
IAF to FAF			
FAF to MDA/DH			
Level Off at MDA			
Missed Approach			

LOCAL AIRPORT(S) WORKSHEET

Airport Name _____ _____ _____ _____ _____

Identifier _____ _____ _____ _____ _____

Elevation _____ _____ _____ _____ _____

ATIS _____ _____ _____ _____ _____

Ground _____ _____ _____ _____ _____

Tower/CTAF _____ _____ _____ _____ _____

Approach control _____ _____ _____ _____ _____

Runway _____ _____ _____ _____ _____

  Approach(es) _____ _____ _____ _____ _____

  Length _____ _____ _____ _____ _____

  Traffic Pattern | Left or Right | Left or Right | Left or Right | Left or Right | Left or Right

  Obstructions _____ _____ _____ _____ _____

Runway _____ _____ _____ _____ _____

  Approach(es) _____ _____ _____ _____ _____

  Length _____ _____ _____ _____ _____

  Traffic Pattern | Left or Right | Left or Right | Left or Right | Left or Right | Left or Right

  Obstructions _____ _____ _____ _____ _____

Runway _____ _____ _____ _____ _____

  Approach(es) _____ _____ _____ _____ _____

  Length _____ _____ _____ _____ _____

  Traffic Pattern | Left or Right | Left or Right | Left or Right | Left or Right | Left or Right

  Obstructions _____ _____ _____ _____ _____

Runway _____ _____ _____ _____ _____

  Approach(es) _____ _____ _____ _____ _____

  Length _____ _____ _____ _____ _____

  Traffic Pattern | Left or Right | Left or Right | Left or Right | Left or Right | Left or Right

  Obstructions _____ _____ _____ _____ _____

Traffic Pattern Altitude _____ _____ _____ _____ _____

INSTRUMENT RATING SYLLABUS LESSON SEQUENCE AND TIMES

> The Ground Syllabus follows on pages 15 through 34 and the Flight Syllabus follows on pages 37 through 70.

The table on the following pages lists the sequence of the flight and ground lessons and the minimum time for each lesson. The times listed are for instructor/student guidance only and are not meant to be mandatory times. These times will ensure that the minimum time requirements for aeronautical knowledge and flight training are in compliance with Part 141, Appendix C, Instrument Rating Course.

14 CFR 61.65, Instrument rating requirements, requires that you have logged at least 50 hours of cross-country time as pilot in command (of which 10 hours must be in an airplane). A total of 40 hours of actual or simulated instrument time in the areas of operation listed in 14 CFR 61.65(c) is required, of which 15 hours must have been received from an authorized instructor. This instrument time must include 3 hours of instrument flight training within 2 calendar months before the date of the practical test and a 250 NM IFR cross-country flight with a total of 3 approaches. Thus, if you are conducting your training under Part 61, you and your instructor must add at least 5 additional instrument flight training hours to the 35-hour total in the following table. Additionally, you are responsible for ensuring that you have 50 hours of cross-country time as pilot in command. Gleim leaves the selection of which lessons to add up to the student/instructor to ensure the appropriate content is covered for each student.

Each training flight must include a preflight briefing and a postflight critique of the pilot's performance by the instructor.

If you are using a flight simulation training device or aviation training device, the columns under BATD, AATD, and FFS represent a sample recommended sequence of lessons that can maximize use of simulator time. These are not the only lessons for which a simulator may be used. For more information, including definitions and approvals for the use of various types of simulators under Part 61 or 141, refer to Appendix B, starting on page 111.

		Flight					Ground
LESSON	Page	Instrument Flight Training	Dual Cross-Country	BATD	AATD	FFS	Aeronautical Knowledge Training
STAGE ONE							
Flight 1 Attitude Instrument Flying	40	1.0		0.75	1.0	1.0	
Ground 1 Airplane Instruments	18						2.0

Flight 2
  Instrument Takeoff/Steep Turns/
  Airspeed Changes
	41	1.0					

Ground 2
  Attitude Instrument Flying/
  Aerodynamics
	19						2.0

Flight 3
  Rate Climbs/Descents, Timed
  Turns/Magnetic Compass Turns
	42	1.0			1.0	1.0	

Flight 4 Partial-Panel Flying	43	1.0			1.0	1.0	

Flight 5
  Attitude Instrument Flying
  (Review)
	44	1.0					

Flight 6 Partial-Panel Flying (Review)	45	1.0					
Flight 7 Basic Instrument Flight Patterns	46	1.0				1.0	
Ground 3 Navigation Systems	20						2.0
Flight 8 VOR/VORTAC Procedures	47	1.0		1.0	1.0	1.0	
Flight 9 VOR Time/Dist., DME Arcs	48	1.0			1.0	1.0	
Ground 4 Federal Aviation Regulations	21						2.0
Flight 10 GPS Procedures	49	1.0		1.0	1.0	1.0	
Flight 11 GPS Procedures Advanced	50	1.0			1.0	1.0	
Ground Stage One Knowledge Test	22						1.0
Flight 12 Tracking the Localizer	51	1.0				1.0	
Flight 13 Stage One Check	52	1.5					

LESSON	Page	Flight					Ground
		Instrument Flight Training	Dual Cross-Country	BATD	AATD	FFS	Aeronautical Knowledge Training
STAGE TWO							
Ground 5 Airports/ATC/Airspace	24						2.5
Ground 6 Holding and Instrument Approaches	25						3.0
Flight 14 VOR Holding	54	1.0		1.0	1.0	1.0	
Flight 15 GPS Holding	55	1.0		1.0	1.0	1.0	
Flight 16 Localizer Holding	56	1.0				1.0	
Flight 17 DME and Intersection Holding	57	1.0			1.0	1.0	
Ground 7 Aeromedical Factors	26						1.5
Flight 18 VOR Instrument Approach	58	1.0			1.0	1.0	
Flight 19 GPS Instrument Approaches	59	1.0		1.5	1.5	1.5	
Flight 20 Localizer Instrument Approach	60	1.0				1.0	
Flight 21 ILS Instrument Approach	61	1.0		1.5	1.5	1.0	
Flight 22 Instrument Approaches (Review)	62	1.5					
Ground Stage Two Knowledge Test	27						1.0
Flight 23 Stage Two Check	63	1.0					

		Flight					Ground
LESSON	Page	Instrument Flight Training	Dual Cross-Country	BATD	AATD	FFS	Aeronautical Knowledge Training
STAGE THREE							
Ground 8 Aviation Weather	29						2.5
Ground 9 Aviation Weather Services	30						2.0
Flight 24 Cross-Country and Emergency Procedures	65	2.0	2.0				
Ground 10 IFR En Route	31						2.0
Flight 25 Cross-Country Procedures	66	2.0	2.0				
Ground 11 IFR Flights	32						3.0
Flight 26 Cross-Country Procedures	67	3.0	3.0				
Ground Stage Three Knowledge Test	33						1.0
Flight 27 Maneuvers Review	68	1.0					
Ground End-of-Course Knowledge Test	34						2.5
Flight 28 Stage Three Check	69	1.5					
Flight 29 End-of-Course Test	70	1.5					
TOTALS (PART 141)		35.0	7.0	8.75	14.0	17.5	30.0
TOTALS (PART 61)*		40.0	7.0	10.00	20.0	20.0	
		Min		**Max**	**Max**	**Max**	**Min**

*Part 61 must add at least 5 additional hours to the Part 141 instrument flight training time.

Visit the **G**LEIM® website for free updates,
which are available until the next edition is published.

GleimAviation.com/updates

INSTRUMENT RATING
GROUND TRAINING SYLLABUS
AIRPLANE SINGLE-ENGINE LAND

GROUND TRAINING COURSE OBJECTIVES

The pilot will obtain the necessary aeronautical knowledge and meet the prerequisites specified in Appendix C to 14 CFR Part 141 (and 14 CFR 61.65) to successfully pass the instrument rating (airplane) knowledge test.

GROUND TRAINING COURSE COMPLETION STANDARDS

The pilot will demonstrate through stage knowledge tests and school records that (s)he meets the prerequisites specified in Appendix C to 14 CFR Part 141 (and 14 CFR 61.65) and has the aeronautical knowledge necessary to pass the instrument rating (airplane) knowledge test.

Lesson	Topic	Min. Time in Hours
	Stage One	
1	Airplane Instruments	2.0
2	Attitude Instrument Flying and Aerodynamics	2.0
3	Navigation Systems	2.0
4	Federal Aviation Regulations	2.0
	Stage One Knowledge Test	1.0
	Stage Two	
5	Airports, Air Traffic Control, and Airspace	2.5
6	Holding and Instrument Approaches	3.0
7	Aeromedical Factors	1.5
	Stage Two Knowledge Test	1.0
	Stage Three	
8	Aviation Weather	2.5
9	Aviation Weather Services	2.0
10	IFR En Route	2.0
11	IFR Flights	3.0
	Stage Three Knowledge Test	1.0
	End-of-Course Knowledge Test	2.5
	Total Ground Training	30.0

STAGE ONE

Stage One Objective

To develop the pilot's knowledge of basic attitude instrument flying. The pilot will learn about the operation of various airplane instruments, aerodynamic factors related to instrument flying, and various navigation systems. Finally, the pilot will become familiar with pertinent federal regulations for IFR flight operations.

Stage One Completion Standards

Stage One will have been successfully completed when the pilot passes the Stage One knowledge test with a minimum passing grade of 80%.

Lesson	Topic	Min. Time
1	Airplane Instruments	2.0
2	Attitude Instrument Flying and Aerodynamics	2.0
3	Navigation Systems	2.0
4	Federal Aviation Regulations	2.0
	Stage One Knowledge Test	1.0

GROUND LESSON 1: AIRPLANE INSTRUMENTS

Objective

To develop the pilot's knowledge of the airplane instruments related to instrument flying.

Text References

Instrument Pilot Flight Maneuvers and Practical Test Prep
Instrument Pilot FAA Knowledge Test Prep, Study Unit 1, "Airplane Instruments"

Instrument Pilot Flight Maneuvers and Practical Test Prep Reading Assignment	*Instrument Pilot FAA Knowledge Test Prep* Study Unit 1 Contents
Study Unit 8, "Airplane Flight Instruments and Navigation Equipment" Study Unit 12, "Instrument Flight"	1.1 Compass Errors 1.2 Pitot-Static System 1.3 Altimeter 1.4 Gyroscopes 1.5 Heading Indicator 1.6 Attitude Indicator 1.7 Turn-and-Slip Indicator 1.8 Turn Coordinator (TC) 1.9 Glass Cockpits

Completion Standards

The lesson will have been successfully completed when the pilot answers the questions in Study Unit 1, "Airplane Instruments," of *Instrument Pilot FAA Knowledge Test Prep*, FAA Test Prep Online, and/or Online Ground School with a minimum passing grade of 80%.

	Dates Studied	Date Completed
Instrument Pilot Flight Maneuvers and Practical Test Prep	___ ___ ___ ___ ___	___
Instrument Pilot FAA Knowledge Test Prep	___ ___ ___ ___ ___	___

Notes:

GROUND LESSON 2: ATTITUDE INSTRUMENT FLYING AND AERODYNAMICS

Objective

To develop the pilot's knowledge of attitude instrument flying and the aerodynamic factors related to instrument flying.

Text References

Instrument Pilot Flight Maneuvers and Practical Test Prep
Instrument Pilot FAA Knowledge Test Prep, Study Unit 2, "Attitude Instrument Flying and Aerodynamics"

Instrument Pilot Flight Maneuvers and Practical Test Prep Reading Assignment	*Instrument Pilot FAA Knowledge Test Prep* Study Unit 2 Contents
Study Unit 12, "Instrument Flight" Study Unit 13, "Recovery from Unusual Flight Attitudes" Study Unit 22, "Approach with Loss of Primary Flight Instrument Indicators"	2.1 Turns 2.2 Turn Rates 2.3 Climbs and Descents 2.4 Fundamental Instrument Skills 2.5 Appropriate Instruments for IFR 2.6 Unusual Attitudes 2.7 Inoperative Instruments 2.8 Turbulence and Wind Shear 2.9 Hydroplaning

Completion Standards

The lesson will have been successfully completed when the pilot answers the questions in Study Unit 2, "Attitude Instrument Flying and Aerodynamics," of *Instrument Pilot FAA Knowledge Test Prep*, FAA Test Prep Online, and/or Online Ground School with a minimum passing grade of 80%.

	Dates Studied	Date Completed
Instrument Pilot Flight Maneuvers and Practical Test Prep	⎯⎯ ⎯⎯ ⎯⎯ ⎯⎯ ⎯⎯	⎯⎯
Instrument Pilot FAA Knowledge Test Prep	⎯⎯ ⎯⎯ ⎯⎯ ⎯⎯ ⎯⎯	⎯⎯

Notes:

GROUND LESSON 3: NAVIGATION SYSTEMS

Objective

To further develop the pilot's knowledge of various navigation systems used during IFR flight operations.

Text References

Instrument Pilot Flight Maneuvers and Practical Test Prep
FAR/AIM
Instrument Pilot FAA Knowledge Test Prep, Study Unit 3, "Navigation Systems"

Instrument Pilot Flight Maneuvers and Practical Test Prep Reading Assignment	*Instrument Pilot FAA Knowledge Test Prep* Study Unit 3 Contents
Study Unit 8, "Airplane Flight Instruments and Navigation Equipment" Study Unit 9, "Instrument Flight Deck Check" Study Unit 14, "Intercepting and Tracking Navigational Systems and Arcs"	3.1 Distance Measuring Equipment (DME) 3.2 VOR Receiver Check 3.3 Very High Frequency Omnidirectional Range (VOR) Station 3.4 Horizontal Situation Indicator (HSI) 3.5 HSI/Localizer 3.6 Global Positioning System (GPS) 3.7 Autopilots
FAR/AIM Additional Reference	
AIM Chapter 1. Air Navigation	

Completion Standards

The lesson will have been successfully completed when the pilot answers the questions in Study Unit 3, "Navigation Systems," of *Instrument Pilot FAA Knowledge Test Prep*, FAA Test Prep Online, and/or Online Ground School with a minimum passing grade of 80%.

	Dates Studied	Date Completed
Instrument Pilot Flight Maneuvers and Practical Test Prep	___ ___ ___ ___ ___	___
FAR/AIM	___ ___ ___ ___ ___	___
Instrument Pilot FAA Knowledge Test Prep	___ ___ ___ ___ ___	___

Notes:

GROUND LESSON 4: FEDERAL AVIATION REGULATIONS

Objective

To develop the pilot's knowledge of pertinent federal regulations for IFR flight operations.

Text References

Instrument Pilot Flight Maneuvers and Practical Test Prep
FAR/AIM
Instrument Pilot FAA Knowledge Test Prep, Study Unit 4, "Federal Aviation Regulations"

Instrument Pilot Flight Maneuvers and Practical Test Prep Reading Assignment		*Instrument Pilot FAA Knowledge Test Prep* Study Unit 4 Contents
Study Unit 4, "Pilot Qualifications"		4.1 14 CFR Part 1 4.2 14 CFR Part 61 4.3 14 CFR Part 91 4.4 NTSB Part 830
FAR/AIM Additional Reference	Sections	
14 CFR Part 61 -- Certification: Pilots, Flight Instructors, and Ground Instructors	Entire Part	
14 CFR Part 91 -- General Operating and Flight Rules	91.1-91.421	
Title 49 -- NTSB Part 830	Entire Part	

Completion Standards

The lesson will have been successfully completed when the pilot answers the questions in Study Unit 4, "Federal Aviation Regulations," of *Instrument Pilot FAA Knowledge Test Prep*, FAA Test Prep Online, and/or Online Ground School with a minimum passing grade of 80%.

	Dates Studied	Date Completed
Instrument Pilot Flight Maneuvers and Practical Test Prep	____ ____ ____ ____ ____	____
FAR/AIM	____ ____ ____ ____ ____	____
Instrument Pilot FAA Knowledge Test Prep	____ ____ ____ ____ ____	____

Notes:

STAGE ONE KNOWLEDGE TEST

Objective

To evaluate the pilot's understanding of the material presented during Ground Lesson 1 through Ground Lesson 4. The Stage One knowledge test consists of 20 questions beginning on page 72.

Content

<u>Lesson</u>

1   Airplane Instruments
2   Attitude Instrument Flying and Aerodynamics
3   Navigation Systems
4   Federal Aviation Regulations

Completion Standards

The lesson will have been successfully completed when the pilot has completed the Stage One knowledge test with a minimum passing grade of 80%.

STAGE TWO

Stage Two Objective

To develop the pilot's knowledge of ATC clearances, holding procedures, and instrument approach procedures and charts. The pilot will learn about airport markings and signs, airspace, and arrival and departure procedures and charts. Additionally, the pilot will learn about aeromedical factors, aeronautical decision making, and crew resource management.

Stage Two Completion Standards

Stage Two will have been successfully completed when the pilot passes the Stage Two knowledge test with a minimum passing grade of 80%.

Lesson	Topic	Min. Time
5	Airports, Air Traffic Control, and Airspace	2.5
6	Holding and Instrument Approaches	3.0
7	Aeromedical Factors	1.5
	Stage Two Knowledge Test	1.0

GROUND LESSON 5: AIRPORTS, AIR TRAFFIC CONTROL, AND AIRSPACE

Objective

To develop the pilot's knowledge of airports, wake turbulence and collision avoidance, ATC communication procedures and phraseology, ATC clearances, IFR flight plan and information, and the National Airspace System.

Text References

Instrument Pilot Flight Maneuvers and Practical Test Prep
FAR/AIM
Instrument Pilot FAA Knowledge Test Prep, Study Unit 5, "Airports, Air Traffic Control, and Airspace"

Instrument Pilot Flight Maneuvers and Practical Test Prep Reading Assignment	*Instrument Pilot FAA Knowledge Test Prep* Study Unit 5 Contents
Study Unit 6, "Cross-Country Flight Planning" Study Unit 10, "Compliance with Air Traffic Control Clearances" Study Unit 15, "Departure, En Route, and Arrival Operations" Study Unit 21, "Loss of Communications"	5.1 Precision Instrument Runway Markings 5.2 Airport Signs and Markings 5.3 Visual Approach Slope Indicator (VASI) 5.4 Precision Approach Path Indicator (PAPI) 5.5 Runway Light Systems 5.6 Wake Turbulence 5.7 Collision Avoidance 5.8 IFR Flight Planning Information 5.9 IFR Flight Plan
FAR/AIM Additional Reference	5.10 ATC Clearances
AIM Chapter 2. Aeronautical Lighting and Other Airport Visual Aids *AIM* Chapter 3. Airspace *AIM* Chapter 4. Air Traffic Control *AIM* Chapter 5. Air Traffic Procedures	5.11 ATC Communication Procedures 5.12 Radio Communication Failure 5.13 Navigation Radio Failure 5.14 Airspace 5.15 Airport Diagram – Chart Supplement

Completion Standards

The lesson will have been successfully completed when the pilot answers the questions in Study Unit 5, "Airports, Air Traffic Control, and Airspace," of *Instrument Pilot FAA Knowledge Test Prep*, FAA Test Prep Online, and/or Online Ground School with a minimum passing grade of 80%.

	Dates Studied	Date Completed
Instrument Pilot Flight Maneuvers and Practical Test Prep	___ ___ ___ ___ ___	___
FAR/AIM	___ ___ ___ ___ ___	___
Instrument Pilot FAA Knowledge Test Prep	___ ___ ___ ___ ___	___

Notes:

GROUND LESSON 6: HOLDING AND INSTRUMENT APPROACHES

Objective

To develop the pilot's knowledge of holding procedures and instrument approach procedures. Additionally, the pilot will learn about standard terminal arrival route (STAR) procedures and instrument departure procedures (DP).

Text References

Instrument Pilot Flight Maneuvers and Practical Test Prep
FAR/AIM
Instrument Pilot FAA Knowledge Test Prep, Study Unit 6, "Holding and Instrument Approaches"

Instrument Pilot Flight Maneuvers and Practical Test Prep Reading Assignment	*Instrument Pilot FAA Knowledge Test Prep* Study Unit 6 Contents
Study Unit 11, "Holding Procedures" Study Unit 15, "Departure, En Route, and Arrival Operations" Part II, Section VI (Introduction) Study Unit 16, "Nonprecision Approach" Study Unit 17, "Precision Approach" Study Unit 18, "Missed Approach" Study Unit 19, "Circling Approach" Study Unit 20, "Landing from an Instrument Approach"	6.1 Contact and Visual Approaches 6.2 Precision Runway Monitor (PRM) 6.3 Runway Visual Range (RVR) 6.4 Missed Approaches 6.5 ILS Specifications 6.6 Unusable ILS Components 6.7 Flying the Approach 6.8 Side-Step Approaches 6.9 Holding 6.10 Instrument Approach Charts 6.11 DPs and STARs 6.12 GPS Approaches
FAR/AIM Additional Reference	
AIM Chapter 5. Air Traffic Procedures	

Completion Standards

The lesson will have been successfully completed when the pilot answers the questions in Study Unit 6, "Holding and Instrument Approaches," of *Instrument Pilot FAA Knowledge Test Prep*, FAA Test Prep Online, and/or Online Ground School with a minimum passing grade of 80%.

	Dates Studied	Date Completed
Instrument Pilot Flight Maneuvers and Practical Test Prep	____ ____ ____ ____ ____	____
FAR/AIM	____ ____ ____ ____ ____	____
Instrument Pilot FAA Knowledge Test Prep	____ ____ ____ ____ ____	____

Notes:

GROUND LESSON 7: AEROMEDICAL FACTORS

Objective

To further develop the pilot's knowledge of the medical factors related to instrument flight, the aeronautical decision-making (ADM) process, and crew resource management.

Text References

Pilot Handbook
Instrument Pilot Flight Maneuvers and Practical Test Prep
FAR/AIM
Instrument Pilot FAA Knowledge Test Prep, Study Unit 7, "Aeromedical Factors"

Pilot Handbook Reading Assignment	*Instrument Pilot FAA Knowledge Test Prep* Study Unit 7 Contents
Study Unit 6, "Aeromedical Factors and Aeronautical Decision Making (ADM)"	7.1 Hypoxia and Hyperventilation 7.2 Spatial Disorientation 7.3 Vision and Visual Illusion 7.4 Fatigue
Instrument Pilot Flight Maneuvers and Practical Test Prep Reading Assignment	
Appendix A, "Risk Management Overview"	
FAR/AIM Additional Reference	
AIM Chapter 8. Medical Facts for Pilots	

Completion Standards

The lesson will have been successfully completed when the pilot answers the questions in Study Unit 7, "Aeromedical Factors," of *Instrument Pilot FAA Knowledge Test Prep*, FAA Test Prep Online, and/or Online Ground School with a minimum passing grade of 80%.

	Dates Studied	Date Completed
Pilot Handbook	____ ____ ____ ____ ____	____
Instrument Pilot Flight Maneuvers and Practical Test Prep	____ ____ ____ ____ ____	____
FAR/AIM	____ ____ ____ ____ ____	____
Instrument Pilot FAA Knowledge Test Prep	____ ____ ____ ____ ____	____

Notes:

STAGE TWO KNOWLEDGE TEST

Objective

To evaluate the pilot's understanding of the material presented during Ground Lesson 5 through Ground Lesson 7. The Stage Two knowledge test consists of 20 questions beginning on page 74.

Content

<u>Lesson</u>

5   Airports, Air Traffic Control, and Airspace
6   Holding and Instrument Approaches
7   Aeromedical Factors

Completion Standards

The lesson will have been successfully completed when the pilot has completed the Stage Two knowledge test with a minimum passing grade of 80%.

STAGE THREE

Stage Three Objective

To develop the pilot's knowledge of IFR cross-country flights. The pilot will learn about weather theory as well as how to use aviation weather reports and forecasts, including how to use those items along with personal observations of weather conditions to forecast weather trends. The pilot will learn about IFR en route operations and IFR en route chart interpretation. Finally, the pilot will review previously learned material with a comprehensive review of IFR flights.

Stage Three Completion Standards

Stage Three will have been successfully completed when the pilot passes the Stage Three knowledge test with a minimum passing grade of 80%.

Lesson	Topic	Min. Time
8	Aviation Weather	2.5
9	Aviation Weather Services	2.0
10	IFR En Route	2.0
11	IFR Flights	3.0
	Stage Three Knowledge Test	1.0
	End-of-Course Knowledge Test	2.5

GROUND LESSON 8: AVIATION WEATHER

Objective

To develop the pilot's ability to recognize critical weather situations and avoid wind shear.

Text References

Instrument Pilot Flight Maneuvers and Practical Test Prep
Aviation Weather and Weather Services (Part I)
FAR/AIM
Instrument Pilot FAA Knowledge Test Prep, Study Unit 8, "Aviation Weather"

Instrument Pilot Flight Maneuvers and Practical Test Prep Reading Assignment	*Instrument Pilot FAA Knowledge Test Prep* Study Unit 8 Contents
Study Unit 5, "Weather Information" Study Unit 7, "Airplane Systems Related to IFR Operations"	8.1 Causes of Weather 8.2 Stability of Air Masses 8.3 Temperature Inversions 8.4 Temperature, Dew Point, and Fog 8.5 Clouds 8.6 Thunderstorms 8.7 Icing 8.8 Wind Shear 8.9 Microbursts
Aviation Weather and Weather Services Part I Reading Assignment	
Study Unit 1, "The Earth's Atmosphere" Study Unit 2, "Temperature" Study Unit 3, "Water Vapor" Study Unit 4, "Atmospheric Pressure and Altimetry" Study Unit 5, "Wind" Study Unit 6, "Air Masses, Fronts, and the Wave Cyclone Model" Study Unit 7, "Vertical Motion" Study Unit 8, "Atmospheric Stability" Study Unit 9, "Clouds" Study Unit 10, "Precipitation" Study Unit 11, "Weather, Obstructions to Visibility, Low Ceiling, and Mountain Obscuration" Study Unit 12, "Turbulence" Study Unit 13, "Icing" Study Unit 14, "Thunderstorms"	
FAR/AIM Additional Reference	
AIM Chapter 7. Safety of Flight	

Completion Standards

The lesson will have been successfully completed when the pilot answers the questions in Study Unit 8, "Aviation Weather," of *Instrument Pilot FAA Knowledge Test Prep*, FAA Test Prep Online, and/or Online Ground School with a minimum passing grade of 80%.

	Dates Studied	Date Completed
Instrument Pilot Flight Maneuvers and Practical Test Prep	___ ___ ___ ___ ___ ___	___
Aviation Weather and Weather Services	___ ___ ___ ___ ___ ___	___
FAR/AIM	___ ___ ___ ___ ___ ___	___
Instrument Pilot FAA Knowledge Test Prep	___ ___ ___ ___ ___ ___	___

Notes:

GROUND LESSON 9: AVIATION WEATHER SERVICES

Objective

To develop the pilot's knowledge of procurement and use of aviation weather reports and forecasts, and the elements of forecasting weather trends on the basis of that information and personal observation of weather conditions.

Text References

Aviation Weather and Weather Services (Part II)
FAR/AIM
Instrument Pilot FAA Knowledge Test Prep, Study Unit 9, "Aviation Weather Services"

Aviation Weather and Weather Services Part II Reading Assignment	*Instrument Pilot FAA Knowledge Test Prep* Study Unit 9 Contents
Study Unit 3, "Observations – Aviation Routine Weather Reports (METAR) and Special Weather Reports (SPECI)" Study Unit 4, "Observations – Aircraft Observations and Reports" Study Unit 5, "Observations – Radar Observations" Study Unit 10, "Analysis – Surface Analysis Charts" Study Unit 11, "Analysis – Ceiling and Visibility" Study Unit 12, "Analysis – Upper-Air Analyses" Study Unit 13, "Forecasts – Significant Meteorological Information (SIGMET)" Study Unit 14, "Forecasts – Airmen's Meteorological Information (AIRMET)" Study Unit 15, "Forecasts – Graphical Airman's Meteorological Advisory (G-AIRMET)" Study Unit 16, "Forecasts – Center Weather Advisory (CWA)" Study Unit 18, "Forecasts – Additional Products for Convection" Study Unit 23, "Forecasts – Terminal Aerodrome Forecasts (TAF)" Study Unit 25, "Forecasts – Wind and Temperature Aloft" Study Unit 26, "Forecasts – Freezing-Level Graphics" Study Unit 28, "Forecasts – Short-Range Surface Prognostic (Prog) Charts" Study Unit 29, "Forecasts – Significant Weather (SIGWX) Forecast" Study Unit 31, "Forecasts – Additional Products for Icing and Turbulence"	9.1 AIRMETs and SIGMETs 9.2 Aviation Routine Weather Report (METAR) 9.3 Pilot Weather Reports (PIREPs) 9.4 Terminal Aerodrome Forecast (TAF) 9.5 Winds and Temperatures Aloft Forecast (FB) 9.6 Low-Level Significant Weather Prog 9.7 Graphical Forecasts for Aviation (GFAs) 9.8 High-Level Significant Weather Prog 9.9 In-Flight Weather Advisories 9.10 Miscellaneous Charts and Forecasts
FAR/AIM Additional Reference	
AIM Chapter 7. Safety of Flight	

Completion Standards

The lesson will have been successfully completed when the pilot answers the questions in Study Unit 9, "Aviation Weather Services," of *Instrument Pilot FAA Knowledge Test Prep*, FAA Test Prep Online, and/or Online Ground School with a minimum passing grade of 80%.

	Dates Studied	Date Completed
Aviation Weather and Weather Services	____ ____ ____ ____ ____	____
FAR/AIM	____ ____ ____ ____ ____	____
Instrument Pilot FAA Knowledge Test Prep	____ ____ ____ ____ ____	____

Notes:

GROUND LESSON 10: IFR EN ROUTE

Objective

To develop the pilot's knowledge of IFR en route operations and interpretation of IFR en route charts.

Text References

Instrument Pilot Flight Maneuvers and Practical Test Prep
FAR/AIM
Instrument Pilot FAA Knowledge Test Prep, Study Unit 10, "IFR En Route"

Instrument Pilot Flight Maneuvers and Practical Test Prep Reading Assignment	*Instrument Pilot FAA Knowledge Test Prep* Study Unit 10 Contents
Study Unit 10, "Compliance with Air Traffic Control Clearances" Appendix C, section "IFR Altitudes Defined"	10.1 Minimum IFR Altitudes 10.2 VFR-on-Top 10.3 IFR En Route Chart Interpretation
FAR/AIM Additional Reference	
AIM Chapter 5. Air Traffic Procedures *AIM* Chapter 9. Aeronautical Charts and Related Publications	

Completion Standards

The lesson will have been successfully completed when the pilot answers the questions in Study Unit 10, "IFR En Route," of *Instrument Pilot FAA Knowledge Test Prep*, FAA Test Prep Online, and/or Online Ground School with a minimum passing grade of 80%.

	Dates Studied	Date Completed
Instrument Pilot Flight Maneuvers and Practical Test Prep	⎯ ⎯ ⎯ ⎯ ⎯	⎯
FAR/AIM	⎯ ⎯ ⎯ ⎯ ⎯	⎯
Instrument Pilot FAA Knowledge Test Prep	⎯ ⎯ ⎯ ⎯ ⎯	⎯

Notes:

GROUND LESSON 11: IFR FLIGHTS

Objective

To further develop the pilot's knowledge of basic cross-country flight planning procedures. Additionally, the pilot will review applicable regulations and procedures for IFR flight operations and the use and interpretation of IFR en route and instrument approach procedure charts.

Text References

Instrument Pilot Flight Maneuvers and Practical Test Prep (review as necessary)
FAR/AIM
Instrument Pilot FAA Knowledge Test Prep, Study Unit 11, "IFR Flights"

Instrument Pilot Flight Maneuvers and Practical Test Prep Part II Contents	*Instrument Pilot FAA Knowledge Test Prep* Study Unit 11 Contents
I. Preflight Preparation II. Preflight Procedures III. Air Traffic Control Clearances and Procedures IV. Flight by Reference to Instruments V. Navigation Systems VI. Instrument Approach Procedures VII. Emergency Operations VIII. Postflight Procedures	11.1 GJT to DRO 11.2 MFR to EUG 11.3 YKM to PDX 11.4 SBA to PRB 11.5 HOT to ADS 11.6 21XS to DFW 11.7 4N1 to BDL 11.8 HLN to BIL
FAR/AIM Additional Reference	
AIM Chapter 4. Air Traffic Control *AIM* Chapter 5. Air Traffic Procedures *AIM* Chapter 6. Emergency Procedures	

Completion Standards

The lesson will have been successfully completed when the pilot answers the questions in Study Unit 11, "IFR Flights," of *Instrument Pilot FAA Knowledge Test Prep*, FAA Test Prep Online, and/or Online Ground School with a minimum passing grade of 80%.

––––––––––––––––––––––

	Dates Studied	Date Completed
Instrument Pilot Flight Maneuvers and Practical Test Prep	____ ____ ____ ____ ____	____
FAR/AIM	____ ____ ____ ____ ____	____
Instrument Pilot FAA Knowledge Test Prep	____ ____ ____ ____ ____	____

Notes:

STAGE THREE KNOWLEDGE TEST

Objective

To evaluate the pilot's understanding of the material presented during Ground Lesson 8 through Ground Lesson 11. The Stage Three knowledge test consists of 20 questions beginning on page 76.

Content

Lesson

8	Aviation Weather
9	Aviation Weather Services
10	IFR En Route
11	IFR Flights

Completion Standards

The lesson will have been successfully completed when the pilot has completed the Stage Three knowledge test with a minimum passing grade of 80%.

END-OF-COURSE KNOWLEDGE TEST

Objective

To evaluate the pilot's comprehension of the material covered in the ground training course and to determine the pilot's readiness to take the FAA instrument rating (airplane) knowledge test. The End-of-Course knowledge test consists of 60 questions beginning on page 78.

Content

Practice Instrument Rating Knowledge Test

Completion Standards

The lesson will have been successfully completed when the pilot has completed the practice instrument rating (airplane) knowledge test with a minimum passing grade of 80%.

PILOT AND INSTRUCTOR LOG FOR GROUND TRAINING COMPLETION*

Lesson		Time (Hours)	Initials/Dates Pilot	Instructor
Stage One				
1	Airplane Instruments	2.0	____/____	____/____
2	Attitude Instrument Flying and Aerodynamics	2.0	____/____	____/____
3	Navigation Systems	2.0	____/____	____/____
4	Federal Aviation Regulations	2.0	____/____	____/____
	Stage One Knowledge Test	1.0	____/____	____/____
Stage Two				
5	Airports, Air Traffic Control, and Airspace	2.5	____/____	____/____
6	Holding and Instrument Approaches	3.0	____/____	____/____
7	Aeromedical Factors	1.5	____/____	____/____
	Stage Two Knowledge Test	1.0	____/____	____/____
Stage Three				
8	Aviation Weather	2.5	____/____	____/____
9	Aviation Weather Services	2.0	____/____	____/____
10	IFR En Route	2.0	____/____	____/____
11	IFR Flights	3.0	____/____	____/____
	Stage Three Knowledge Test	1.0	____/____	____/____
	End-of-Course Knowledge Test	2.5	____/____	____/____
	Total Ground Training	30.0		

*Required for Part 141 but NOT required for the authorization form below. A CFII or IGI (instrument ground instructor) can endorse (or "sign off") the authorization form below, based on the individual's assertion that (s)he studied Gleim.

NOTE: You may also use the Instrument Pilot Training Record to log this information.

INSTRUCTOR AUTHORIZATION FORM
INSTRUMENT RATING KNOWLEDGE TEST

Name: _____

    I certify that I have reviewed the above individual's preparation for the FAA Instrument Rating–Airplane knowledge test [covering the topics specified in Appendix C to 14 CFR Part 141**] using the *Instrument Pilot FAA Knowledge Test Prep* book, FAA Test Prep Online, and/or Online Ground School course by Irvin N. Gleim and Garrett W. Gleim and find him or her competent to pass the knowledge test.

**Also the topics specified in 14 CFR 61.65(b)(1) through (10).

_____ _____ _____ _____ _____
Signed   Date   Name   CFII/IGI Number CFI Exp. Date

When completed, make one copy to take to the knowledge test center AND one copy for your CFII/IGI/flight school.

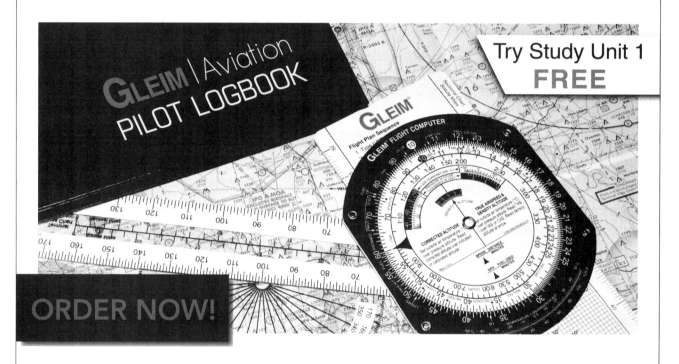

INSTRUMENT RATING
FLIGHT TRAINING SYLLABUS
AIRPLANE SINGLE-ENGINE LAND

FLIGHT TRAINING COURSE OBJECTIVES

The pilot will obtain the aeronautical knowledge and experience and demonstrate the flight proficiency necessary to meet the requirements for an instrument rating with an airplane category rating.

FLIGHT TRAINING COURSE COMPLETION STANDARDS

The pilot will demonstrate through the stage checks and school records that (s)he has the necessary flight proficiency and aeronautical experience to obtain an instrument rating with an airplane category rating.

The following is a brief description of the parts of each flight lesson in this syllabus:

Objective: We open each lesson with an objective, usually a sentence or two, to help you gain perspective and understand the goal for that particular lesson.

Text References: For lessons with new learning items, this section tells you which reference books you will need to study or refer to while mastering the tasks within the lesson. Abbreviations are given to facilitate the cross-referencing process.

Content: Each lesson contains a list of the tasks required to be completed before moving to the next lesson. A task may be listed as a "review item" (a task that was covered in a previous lesson) or as a "new item" (a task that is introduced to you for the first time). Each task is preceded by three blank "checkoff" boxes, which may be used by your CFI to keep track of your progress and to indicate that each task was completed.

There are three boxes because it may take more than one flight to complete the lesson. Your CFI may mark the box(es) next to each task in one of the following methods (or any other method desired):

✓ - task completed to lesson completion standards	D - demonstrated by instructor A - accomplished by you S - safe/satisfactory C - meets or exceeds ACS standards	1 - above lesson standard 2 - meets lesson standard 3 - below lesson standard

The last task in each flight lesson is labeled "Additional items at CFI's discretion," and is followed by several blank lines. This area can be used to record any extra items that your CFI feels are appropriate to the lesson, taking into account such variables as weather, local operational considerations, and your progress as a student.

NOTE: CFIs are reminded not to limit themselves to the blank lines provided–use as much of the page as you need.

Completion Standards: Based on these standards, your CFI determines how well you have met the objective of the lesson in terms of knowledge and skill.

Instructor's Comments and Lesson Assignment: Space is provided for your CFI's critique of the lesson, which you can refer to later. Your instructor may also write any specific assignment for the next lesson.

Reading Assignments for Flight Lessons

You are expected to be prepared for each flight lesson. Our reading assignments include text references for new tasks to help you understand what is going to happen and how and why you need to do everything **before** you go to the airport.

Next to each new item in the **Content** section, we provide study unit-level references to read in *Instrument Pilot Flight Maneuvers and Practical Test Prep* (FM) and the section to read, if appropriate, in your airplane's Pilot's Operating Handbook (POH). You can make use of the comprehensive index in the Gleim books if you need to analyze specific task element-level details.

Study Tips

- As you read the material, attempt to understand the basic concepts.
- Try to anticipate and visualize the concepts and flight maneuvers.
- With this basic knowledge, your CFI can expand on the specific and finer points, especially when explaining how a task is done in your specific airplane.
- After your flight lesson, task items are fresh in your mind; they will make sense, and you should be able to understand and learn more.
- Study review items so you can explain them to your CFI and your examiner.
- After you study, relax and plan a time to begin preparing for the next flight lesson.

STAGE ONE

Stage One Objective

The pilot will be able to precisely control the airplane using basic attitude instrument flying skills and the airplane's navigation systems.

Stage One Completion Standards

The stage will be completed when the pilot satisfactorily passes the Stage One check and is able to precisely control the airplane using basic attitude instrument flying skills under full- and partial-panel instrument panel conditions. Additionally, the pilot will be able to fly a predetermined course using the airplane's navigation systems.

Lesson	Topic
	Stage One
1	Attitude Instrument Flying
2	Instrument Takeoff, Steep Turns, and Airspeed Changes
3	Rate Climbs/Descents, Timed Turns, and Magnetic Compass Turns
4	Partial-Panel Flying
5	Attitude Instrument Flying (review)
6	Partial-Panel Flying (review)
7	Basic Instrument Flight Patterns
8	VOR/VORTAC Procedures
9	VOR Time/Distance to Station and DME Arcs
10	GPS Procedures
11	GPS Procedures Advanced
12	Tracking the Localizer
13	Stage One Check

FLIGHT LESSON 1: ATTITUDE INSTRUMENT FLYING

FSTD/ATD option

Objective

To introduce basic attitude instrument flying and to develop the pilot's proficiency and confidence in flying the airplane solely by reference to instruments.

Text References

Instrument Pilot Flight Maneuvers and Practical Test Prep (FM)
Pilot's Operating Handbook (POH)

Content

1. Preflight briefing
2. New items
   - ☐☐☐ Attitude instrument flying - FM 12
   - ☐☐☐ Airplane flight instruments - FM 12; POH 7
   - ☐☐☐ Straight-and-level flight - FM 12
   - ☐☐☐ Change of airspeed - FM 12
   - ☐☐☐ Constant airspeed climbs and descents - FM 12
   - ☐☐☐ Standard rate turns - CFII
   - ☐☐☐ Maneuvering during slow flight - CFII
   - ☐☐☐ Power-off stall - CFII
   - ☐☐☐ Power-on stall - CFII
   - ☐☐☐ Recovery from unusual flight attitudes - FM 13
   - ☐☐☐ Use of checklists - POH 4
   - ☐☐☐ Radio communications - CFII
   - ☐☐☐ Additional items at CFI's discretion _____

   _____

3. Postflight critique and preview of next lesson

Completion Standards

The lesson will have been successfully completed when the pilot demonstrates an understanding of attitude instrument flying as related to airplane control. The pilot will maintain airplane control at all times and maintain the desired altitude, ±200 ft.; airspeed, ±10 kt.; and heading, ±15°.

Instructor's comments: _____

_____

Lesson assignment: _____

_____

Notes: _____

_____

_____

_____

_____

_____

_____

_____

_____

_____

_____

FLIGHT LESSON 2: INSTRUMENT TAKEOFF, STEEP TURNS, AND AIRSPEED CHANGES

FSTD/ATD option

Objective

To introduce the pilot to IFR preflight, instrument takeoff, change of airspeed, steep turns, and postflight procedures and to increase the pilot's proficiency in attitude instrument flying.

Text References

Instrument Pilot Flight Maneuvers and Practical Test Prep (FM)
Pilot's Operating Handbook (POH)

Content

1. Flight Lesson 1 complete? Yes ____   Copy of lesson placed in pilot's folder? Yes ____
2. Preflight briefing
3. Review items
   - ☐☐☐ Airplane flight instruments
   - ☐☐☐ Use of checklists
   - ☐☐☐ Radio communications
   - ☐☐☐ Attitude instrument flying
   - ☐☐☐ Straight-and-level flight
   - ☐☐☐ Change of airspeed
   - ☐☐☐ Standard rate turns
   - ☐☐☐ Constant airspeed climbs and descents
   - ☐☐☐ Recovery from unusual flight attitudes
   - ☐☐☐ Maneuvering during slow flight
   - ☐☐☐ Power-off stall
   - ☐☐☐ Power-on stall
   _____

4. New items
   - ☐☐☐ IFR preflight inspection - CFII
   - ☐☐☐ Preflight procedures - FM 7-9
   - ☐☐☐ Airplane systems related to IFR operations - FM 7
   - ☐☐☐ Airplane navigation equipment - FM 8; POH 9
   - ☐☐☐ Instrument flight deck check - FM 9
   - ☐☐☐ Instrument takeoff - FM App D
   - ☐☐☐ Steep turns - CFII
   - ☐☐☐ IFR postflight procedures - FM 23
   - ☐☐☐ Additional items at CFI's discretion _____
   _____

5. Postflight critique and preview of next lesson

Completion Standards

The lesson will have been successfully completed when the pilot displays an understanding of IFR preflight and postflight procedures, the instrument flight deck check, and the instrument takeoff procedures. The pilot will demonstrate increased proficiency in attitude instrument flying. The pilot will be able to maintain the desired altitude, ±200 ft.; airspeed, ±10 kt.; and heading, ±15°.

Instructor's comments: _____

_____

Lesson assignment: _____

_____

Notes: _____

_____

_____

FLIGHT LESSON 3: RATE CLIMBS/DESCENTS, TIMED TURNS, AND MAGNETIC COMPASS TURNS

FSTD/ATD option

Objective

To introduce the pilot to constant rate climbs and descents, timed turns to magnetic compass headings, and magnetic compass turns. Additionally, this lesson will increase the pilot's proficiency in attitude instrument flying.

Text References

Instrument Pilot Flight Maneuvers and Practical Test Prep (FM)

Content

1. Flight Lesson 2 complete? Yes ____   Copy of lesson placed in pilot's folder? Yes ____
2. Preflight briefing
3. Review items
   - ☐☐☐ IFR preflight inspection
   - ☐☐☐ Airplane systems related to IFR operations
   - ☐☐☐ Airplane flight instruments and navigation equipment
   - ☐☐☐ Instrument flight deck check
   - ☐☐☐ Straight-and-level flight
   - ☐☐☐ Standard rate turns
   - ☐☐☐ Recovery from unusual flight attitudes
   - ☐☐☐ Slow flight
   - ☐☐☐ Power-off stall
   - ☐☐☐ Steep turns
   - ☐☐☐ IFR postflight procedures
   _____

4. New items
   - ☐☐☐ Rate climbs and descents - FM 12
   - ☐☐☐ Timed turns to magnetic compass headings - FM 12
   - ☐☐☐ Magnetic compass turns - FM 12
   - ☐☐☐ Additional items at CFI's discretion _____
   _____

5. Postflight critique and preview of next lesson

Completion Standards

The lesson will have been successfully completed when the pilot displays an understanding of how to perform rate climbs and descents, calibrate the turn coordinator for timed turns, and make turns to headings by use of a timed turn or the magnetic compass. Additionally, the pilot will demonstrate increased proficiency in attitude instrument flying. The pilot will be able to maintain the desired altitude, ±150 ft.; airspeed, ±10 kt.; and heading, ±15°.

Instructor's comments: _____

_____

Lesson assignment: _____

_____

Notes: _____

_____

_____

_____

_____

FLIGHT LESSON 4: PARTIAL-PANEL FLYING

FSTD/ATD option

Objective

To introduce the pilot to partial-panel attitude instrument flying and to increase the pilot's proficiency in constant rate climbs and descents, timed turns, and magnetic compass turns.

Text References

Instrument Pilot Flight Maneuvers and Practical Test Prep (FM)

Content

1. Flight Lesson 3 complete? Yes ____   Copy of lesson placed in pilot's folder? Yes ____
2. Preflight briefing
3. Review items (full panel)
   □□□ Rate climbs and descents
   □□□ Timed turns to magnetic compass headings
   □□□ Magnetic compass turns
   _____

4. New items
   □□□ Loss of primary flight instrument indicators - FM 12, 22
   □□□ Straight-and-level flight (partial panel) - FM 12
   □□□ Magnetic compass turns (partial panel) - FM 12
   □□□ Constant airspeed climbs and descents (partial panel) - FM 12
   □□□ Rate climbs and descents (partial panel) - FM 12
   □□□ Additional items at CFI's discretion _____
   _____

5. Postflight critique and preview of next lesson

Completion Standards

The lesson will have been successfully completed when the pilot demonstrates an understanding of the skills required to maintain airplane control while conducting partial-panel attitude instrument flight. Additionally, the pilot will demonstrate increased proficiency in constant rate climbs and descents, timed turns, and magnetic compass turns. The pilot will be able to maintain the desired altitude, ±150 ft.; airspeed, ±10 kt.; heading, ±15°; and climb/descent rate, ±200 fpm; and to roll out on the desired heading, ±15°.

Instructor's comments: _____

_____

Lesson assignment: _____

_____

Notes: _____

_____

_____

_____

_____

_____

_____

_____

FLIGHT LESSON 5: ATTITUDE INSTRUMENT FLYING (REVIEW)

FSTD/ATD option

Objective

To review previous lessons to gain proficiency in full- and partial-panel attitude instrument flying.

Content

1. Flight Lesson 4 complete? Yes ___   Copy of lesson placed in pilot's folder? Yes ___
2. Preflight briefing
3. Review items

    a. Full-panel attitude instrument flight

        ☐☐☐ IFR preflight inspection
        ☐☐☐ Airplane systems related to IFR operations
        ☐☐☐ Airplane flight instruments and navigation equipment
        ☐☐☐ Instrument flight deck check
        ☐☐☐ Instrument takeoff
        ☐☐☐ Straight-and-level flight
        ☐☐☐ Constant airspeed climbs and descents
        ☐☐☐ Rate climbs and descents
        ☐☐☐ Standard rate turns
        ☐☐☐ Steep turns
        ☐☐☐ Change of airspeed
        ☐☐☐ Maneuvering during slow flight
        ☐☐☐ Stalls
        ☐☐☐ Recovery from unusual flight attitudes
        ☐☐☐ IFR postflight procedures

    b. Partial-panel attitude instrument flight

        ☐☐☐ Straight-and-level flight
        ☐☐☐ Magnetic compass turns
        ☐☐☐ Constant airspeed climbs and descents
        ☐☐☐ Rate climbs and descents

4. Postflight critique and preview of next lesson

Completion Standards

The lesson will have been successfully completed when the pilot demonstrates smooth, coordinated control of the airplane during full-panel attitude instrument flight. Additionally, the pilot will demonstrate increased understanding of partial-panel operations. The pilot will be able to maintain the desired altitude, ±150 ft.; airspeed, ±10 kt.; heading, ±15°; angle of bank, ±5°; and climb/descent rate, ±200 fpm; to roll out on the desired heading, ±15°; and to level off at the desired altitude, ±150 ft. Recovery procedures from stalls and unusual attitudes should be done correctly, with the successful outcome never in doubt.

Instructor's comments: _____

_____

Lesson assignment: _____

_____

Notes: _____

_____

_____

_____

_____

FLIGHT LESSON 6: PARTIAL-PANEL FLYING (REVIEW)

FSTD/ATD option

Objective

To increase the pilot's proficiency in partial-panel attitude instrument flying and to introduce the pilot to more complex partial-panel procedures.

Text References

Instrument Pilot Flight Maneuvers and Practical Test Prep (FM)

Content

1. Flight Lesson 5 complete? Yes ___   Copy of lesson placed in pilot's folder? Yes ___
2. Preflight briefing
3. Review items (partial panel)
   ☐☐☐ Straight-and-level flight
   ☐☐☐ Magnetic compass turns
   ☐☐☐ Constant airspeed climbs and descents
   _____

4. New items (partial panel)
   ☐☐☐ Timed turns to magnetic compass headings - FM 12
   ☐☐☐ Maneuvering during slow flight - CFII
   ☐☐☐ Stalls - CFII
   ☐☐☐ Recovery from unusual flight attitudes - FM 13
   ☐☐☐ Additional items at CFI's discretion _____
   _____

5. Postflight critique and preview of next lesson

Completion Standards

The lesson will have been successfully completed when the pilot displays an understanding of the correct recovery procedures during stalls and unusual attitudes without overcontrolling during partial-panel operations. Additionally, the pilot will demonstrate increased proficiency in partial-panel attitude instrument flight.

Instructor's comments: _____

_____

Lesson assignment: _____

_____

Notes: _____

_____

_____

_____

_____

_____

_____

_____

_____

_____

_____

FLIGHT LESSON 7: BASIC INSTRUMENT FLIGHT PATTERNS

FSTD/ATD option

Objective

To further develop the pilot's ability to precisely control the airplane during attitude instrument flying by combining previously learned maneuvers. This will be accomplished by introducing the pilot to the FAA's various basic instrument flight patterns.

Text References

Instrument Pilot Flight Maneuvers and Practical Test Prep (FM)

Content

1. Flight Lesson 6 complete? Yes ____   Copy of lesson placed in pilot's folder? Yes ____
2. Preflight briefing
3. New items
    - ☐☐☐ Pattern "A" - FM App D
    - ☐☐☐ Pattern "B" - FM App D
    - ☐☐☐ Vertical S - FM App D
    - ☐☐☐ Vertical S-1 - FM App D
    - ☐☐☐ Vertical S-2 - FM App D
    - ☐☐☐ 80/260 procedure turn - FM App D
    - ☐☐☐ Standard procedure turn - FM App D
    - ☐☐☐ Teardrop holding pattern entry - FM App D
    - ☐☐☐ Holding pattern - FM App D
    - ☐☐☐ Patterns applicable to circling approaches - FM App D
    - ☐☐☐ Additional items at CFI's discretion _____

4. Postflight critique and preview of next lesson

Completion Standards

The lesson will have been successfully completed when the pilot displays an understanding of the various basic instrument flight patterns. The pilot will be able to maintain the desired altitude, ±150 ft.; airspeed, ±10 kt.; and heading, ±15°; to roll out on the specified heading, ±15°; and to maintain the desired rate of climb/descent, ±200 fpm.

Instructor's comments: _____

_____

Lesson assignment: _____

_____

Notes: _____

_____

_____

_____

_____

_____

_____

_____

_____

_____

_____

FLIGHT LESSON 8: VOR/VORTAC PROCEDURES

FSTD/ATD option

NOTE: For the remainder of this syllabus, the term VOR will be used to include VOR, VORTAC, and VOR/DME stations.

Objective

To develop the pilot's ability to determine the airplane's position in relation to a VOR station and to intercept and track a predetermined radial.

Text References

Instrument Pilot Flight Maneuvers and Practical Test Prep (FM)

Content

1. Flight Lesson 7 complete? Yes ____   Copy of lesson placed in pilot's folder? Yes ____
2. Preflight briefing
3. Review items
   - ☐☐☐ Constant airspeed climbs and descents
   - ☐☐☐ Pattern "A" (partial panel)
   - ☐☐☐ Vertical S
   - ☐☐☐ Teardrop holding pattern entry
   - ☐☐☐ Recovery from unusual flight attitudes (partial panel)

4. New items
   - ☐☐☐ VOR accuracy test - FM 9
   - ☐☐☐ VOR orientation - FM 8, 9
   - ☐☐☐ Intercepting and tracking a VOR radial - FM 14
   - ☐☐☐ Additional items at CFI's discretion _____

5. Postflight critique and preview of next lesson

Completion Standards

The lesson will have been successfully completed when the pilot displays an understanding of VOR orientation and of intercepting and tracking predetermined radials. Additionally, the pilot will demonstrate increased proficiency in attitude instrument flight. The pilot will be able to maintain the desired altitude, ±150 ft.; airspeed, ±10 kt.; and heading, ±10°.

Instructor's comments: _____

_____

Lesson assignment: _____

_____

Notes: _____

FLIGHT LESSON 9: VOR TIME/DISTANCE TO STATION AND DME ARCS

FSTD/ATD option

Objective

To introduce the pilot to VOR time and distance calculations and the interception and tracking of DME arcs, if the airplane is DME equipped. Additionally, the pilot will gain more proficiency in VOR orientation, radial interception, and tracking.

Text References

Instrument Pilot Flight Maneuvers and Practical Test Prep (FM)

Content

1. Flight Lesson 8 complete? Yes ___   Copy of lesson placed in pilot's folder? Yes ___
2. Preflight briefing
3. Review items
    ☐☐☐ Pattern "B"
    ☐☐☐ Vertical S-2
    ☐☐☐ Holding pattern
    ☐☐☐ VOR accuracy test
    ☐☐☐ VOR orientation
    ☐☐☐ Intercepting and tracking a VOR radial
    _____

4. New items
    ☐☐☐ VOR time and distance calculations - FM App D
    ☐☐☐ Intercepting and tracking DME arcs (if the airplane is DME equipped) - FM 14
    ☐☐☐ Additional items at CFI's discretion _____
    _____

5. Postflight critique and preview of next lesson

Completion Standards

The lesson will have been successfully completed when the pilot can demonstrate an understanding of VOR time and distance calculations and how to intercept and track a DME arc (if the airplane is DME equipped). Additionally, the pilot will demonstrate increased proficiency in VOR orientation, intercepting and tracking VOR radials, and attitude instrument flight. The pilot will be able to maintain the desired altitude, ±100 ft.; airspeed, ±10 kt.; and heading, ±10°; and to track a radial allowing no more than a 3/4-scale deflection of the course deviation indicator (CDI) or remaining within 10° in the case of an RMI.

Instructor's comments: _____

_____

Lesson assignment: _____

_____

Notes: _____

_____

_____

_____

_____

_____

_____

FLIGHT LESSON 10: GPS PROCEDURES

FSTD/ATD option

NOTE: In this lesson and throughout the remainder of this syllabus, any reference to DME arcs or GPS shall be disregarded if the airplane is not equipped with these specified navigational systems.

Objective

To introduce the pilot to GPS orientation and the method used to track a GPS course. Additionally, the pilot will increase proficiency in VOR procedures.

Text References

Instrument Pilot Flight Maneuvers and Practical Test Prep (FM)
Pilot's Operating Handbook (POH)

Content

1. Flight Lesson 9 complete? Yes ___   Copy of lesson placed in pilot's folder? Yes ___
2. Preflight briefing
3. Review items

   ☐☐☐ Basic instrument flight patterns (as directed by your instructor)
   ☐☐☐ VOR orientation
   ☐☐☐ VOR time and distance calculations
   ☐☐☐ Intercepting and tracking VOR radials and arcs
   _____

4. New items

   ☐☐☐ GPS orientation - FM 8
   ☐☐☐ Tracking a GPS course - FM 14
   ☐☐☐ Intercepting a course, tracking, and arcs using GPS - FM 14; POH 9
   ☐☐☐ Additional items at CFI's discretion _____
   _____

5. Postflight critique and preview of next lesson

Completion Standards

The lesson will have been successfully completed when the pilot can demonstrate an understanding of GPS orientation, the method used to track a GPS course, and the method used to intercept, track, and fly an arc using GPS. Additionally, the pilot will demonstrate increased proficiency in VOR procedures. The pilot will be able to maintain the desired altitude, ±100 ft.; airspeed, ±10 kt.; heading, ±10°; and arc, ±2 NM; and to track a VOR radial with no more than a 3/4-scale deflection of the CDI or within 10° in the case of an RMI.

Instructor's comments: _____

_____

Lesson assignment: _____

_____

Notes: _____

_____

_____

_____

_____

_____

_____

FLIGHT LESSON 11: GPS PROCEDURES ADVANCED

FSTD/ATD option

Objective

The pilot will increase proficiency in GPS orientation, tracking a GPS course, and flying an arc using GPS. The pilot will also learn advanced programming functions specific to the equipment installed in their aircraft.

Text References

Instrument Pilot Flight Maneuvers and Practical Test Prep (FM)
Pilot's Operating Handbook (POH)

Content

1. Flight Lesson 10 complete? Yes ____   Copy of lesson placed in pilot's folder? Yes ____
2. Preflight briefing
3. Review items
    ☐☐☐ Basic instrument flight patterns (as directed by your instructor)
    ☐☐☐ GPS orientation
    ☐☐☐ Tracking a GPS course
    ☐☐☐ Intercepting a course, tracking, and arcs using GPS
    _____

4. New items
    ☐☐☐ GPS advanced programming - POH 9
    ☐☐☐ Automation management - FM App A
    ☐☐☐ Additional items at CFI's discretion _____
    _____

5. Postflight critique and preview of next lesson

Completion Standards

The lesson will have been successfully completed when the pilot can demonstrate an understanding of flying an arc using GPS. The pilot will also demonstrate increased proficiency in GPS orientation, tracking a GPS course, and flying an arc using GPS. The pilot will be able to maintain the desired altitude, ±100 ft.; airspeed, ±10 kt.; heading, ±10°; and GPS CDI with no more than 3/4-scale deflection.

Instructor's comments: _____

_____

Lesson assignment: _____

_____

Notes: _____

_____

_____

_____

_____

_____

_____

_____

_____

FLIGHT LESSON 12: TRACKING THE LOCALIZER

FSTD/ATD option

Objective

To introduce the pilot to the procedures to track the localizer. The pilot will also gain more proficiency in VOR, DME, and GPS procedures.

Text References

Instrument Pilot Flight Maneuvers and Practical Test Prep (FM)

Content

1. Flight Lesson 11 complete? Yes ___   Copy of lesson placed in pilot's folder? Yes ___
2. Preflight briefing
3. Review items
    ☐☐☐ Intercepting and tracking VOR radials
    ☐☐☐ Intercepting and tracking DME arcs
    ☐☐☐ Tracking a GPS course
    ☐☐☐ VOR time and distance calculations

4. New items
    ☐☐☐ Tracking the localizer front course - FM 8, 16
    ☐☐☐ Additional items at CFI's discretion ⎯⎯⎯⎯⎯⎯⎯⎯⎯⎯⎯⎯⎯⎯⎯

5. Postflight critique and preview of next lesson

Completion Standards

The lesson will have been successfully completed when the pilot can demonstrate an understanding of front course localizer tracking. The pilot will be able to maintain the desired altitude, ±100 ft.; airspeed, ±10 kt.; heading, ±10°; DME arc, ±2 NM; and to track a VOR radial or a GPS course with no more than a 3/4-scale deflection of the CDI or within 10° in the case of an RMI.

Instructor's comments: ⎯⎯⎯

Lesson assignment: ⎯⎯

Notes: ⎯⎯⎯

FLIGHT LESSON 13: STAGE ONE CHECK

Objective

During this stage check, an authorized flight instructor will determine if the pilot is proficient in attitude instrument flying and in the use of navigation equipment.

Content

1. Flight Lesson 12 complete? Yes ____   Copy of lesson placed in pilot's folder? Yes ____
2. Preflight briefing
3. Stage check tasks

   a. Preflight procedures
   - ☐☐☐ Airplane systems related to IFR operations
   - ☐☐☐ Airplane flight instruments and navigation equipment
   - ☐☐☐ Instrument flight deck check

   _____

   b. Attitude instrument flying -- full and partial panel unless otherwise indicated
   - ☐☐☐ Straight-and-level flight
   - ☐☐☐ Change of airspeed
   - ☐☐☐ Constant airspeed climbs and descents
   - ☐☐☐ Rate climbs and descents
   - ☐☐☐ Timed turns to magnetic compass headings
   - ☐☐☐ Magnetic compass turns (partial panel only)
   - ☐☐☐ Steep turns (full panel only)
   - ☐☐☐ Recovery from unusual flight attitudes

   _____

   c. Navigation systems
   - ☐☐☐ Intercepting and tracking VOR radials
   - ☐☐☐ Intercepting and tracking DME arcs
   - ☐☐☐ Tracking a GPS course
   - ☐☐☐ Tracking a localizer
   - ☐☐☐ Additional items at CFI's discretion _____

   _____

4. Postflight critique and preview of next lesson

Completion Standards

The lesson and Stage One will have been successfully completed when the pilot can demonstrate proficiency in attitude instrument flights (full and partial panel) and navigation procedures. The pilot will be able to maintain the desired altitude, ±100 ft.; airspeed, ±10 kt.; heading, ±5°; rate of climb, ±100 fpm; DME arc, ±2 NM; to roll out on the desired heading, ±10°; and to track a VOR radial or a GPS course with no more than a 3/4-scale deflection of the CDI or within 10° in the case of an RMI.

Instructor's comments: _____

_____

Lesson assignment: _____

_____

Notes: _____

_____

_____

_____

_____

STAGE TWO

Stage Two Objective

The pilot will be introduced to holding procedures and instrument approach procedures, including missed approaches.

Stage Two Completion Standards

The stage will be completed when the pilot demonstrates proficiency in holding procedures using various navigation systems and all types of instrument approach procedures.

Lesson	Topic
	Stage Two
14	VOR Holding
15	GPS Holding
16	Localizer Holding
17	DME and Intersection Holding
18	VOR Instrument Approach
19	GPS Instrument Approaches
20	Localizer Instrument Approach
21	ILS Instrument Approach
22	Instrument Approaches (Review)
23	Stage Two Check

FLIGHT LESSON 14: VOR HOLDING

FSTD/ATD option

Objective

To introduce the pilot to holding procedures at a VOR station, including ATC clearances and holding instructions and holding pattern entry procedures and use of autopilot for holding (if equipped).

Text References

Instrument Pilot Flight Maneuvers and Practical Test Prep (FM)
Pilot's Operating Handbook (POH)

Content

1. Flight Lesson 13 complete? Yes ___   Copy of lesson placed in pilot's folder? Yes ___
2. Preflight briefing
3. Review items
   - ☐☐☐ Airplane systems related to IFR operations
   - ☐☐☐ Instrument flight deck check
   - ☐☐☐ Instrument takeoff
   - ☐☐☐ Intercepting and tracking VOR radials
   - ☐☐☐ Loss of primary flight instrument indicators

4. New items
   - ☐☐☐ Tracking VOR radials (partial panel) - FM 12, 14, 22
   - ☐☐☐ ATC clearances and holding instructions - FM 10, 11
   - ☐☐☐ Holding pattern entry procedures - FM 11
     - ☐☐☐ Parallel procedure
     - ☐☐☐ Teardrop procedure
     - ☐☐☐ Direct entry procedure
   - ☐☐☐ VOR holding procedures - FM 11
     - ☐☐☐ Standard pattern
     - ☐☐☐ Nonstandard pattern
   - ☐☐☐ Use of autopilot for holding (if equipped) - POH 9
   - ☐☐☐ Additional items at CFI's discretion _____

5. Postflight critique and preview of next lesson

Completion Standards

The lesson will have been successfully completed when the pilot can demonstrate an understanding of ATC holding instructions, holding pattern entry procedures, and the procedures to remain in the holding pattern. Additionally, the pilot will demonstrate increased knowledge in systems related to IFR operations and proficiency in the instrument flight deck check and partial-panel instrument flight. The pilot will be able to maintain the desired altitude, ±100 ft.; airspeed, ±10 kt.; and heading, ±10°.

Instructor's comments: _____

_____

Lesson assignment: _____

_____

Notes: _____

_____

_____

_____

FLIGHT LESSON 15: GPS HOLDING

FSTD/ATD option

Objective

To introduce the pilot to GPS holding procedures and use of autopilot for holding (if equipped). Additionally, the pilot will increase proficiency in VOR holding and complying with ATC clearances and holding instructions.

Text References

Instrument Pilot Flight Maneuvers and Practical Test Prep (FM)
Pilot's Operating Handbook (POH)

Content

1. Flight Lesson 14 complete? Yes ____   Copy of lesson placed in pilot's folder? Yes ____
2. Preflight briefing
3. Review items
   - ☐☐☐ ATC clearances and holding instructions
   - ☐☐☐ Holding pattern entry procedures
     - ☐☐☐ Parallel procedure
     - ☐☐☐ Teardrop procedure
     - ☐☐☐ Direct entry procedure
   - ☐☐☐ VOR holding procedures
   - ☐☐☐ Loss of primary flight instrument indicators
   - ☐☐☐ Use of autopilot for holding (if equipped) _____

4. New items
   - ☐☐☐ Tracking GPS courses (partial panel) - FM 14, 22
   - ☐☐☐ GPS holding procedures (if equipped) - FM 11; POH 9
     - ☐☐☐ Standard pattern
     - ☐☐☐ Nonstandard pattern
   - ☐☐☐ Additional items at CFI's discretion _____

5. Postflight critique and preview of next lesson

Completion Standards

The lesson will have been successfully completed when the pilot can demonstrate an understanding of GPS holding procedures. Additionally, the pilot will demonstrate increased proficiency in copying and complying with ATC holding instructions, entries to holding, and VOR holding procedures. The pilot will be able to maintain the desired altitude, ±100 ft.; airspeed, ±10 kt.; and heading, ±10°, and to track a selected course or radial.

Instructor's comments: _____

_____

Lesson assignment: _____

_____

Notes: _____

_____

_____

_____

_____

FLIGHT LESSON 16: LOCALIZER HOLDING

FSTD/ATD option

Objective

To introduce the pilot to localizer holding procedures and use of autopilot for holding (if equipped). Additionally, the pilot will increase proficiency in holding pattern procedures through the practice of VOR and GPS holding.

Text References

Instrument Pilot Flight Maneuvers and Practical Test Prep (FM)

Content

1. Flight Lesson 15 complete? Yes ___   Copy of lesson placed in pilot's folder? Yes ___
2. Preflight briefing
3. Review items
   - ☐☐☐ Airplane systems related to IFR operations
   - ☐☐☐ Instrument flight deck check
   - ☐☐☐ ATC holding instructions
   - ☐☐☐ Holding pattern entry procedures
   - ☐☐☐ VOR holding procedures
   - ☐☐☐ GPS holding procedures
   - ☐☐☐ Use of autopilot for holding (if equipped)

   _____

4. New items
   - ☐☐☐ Localizer holding procedures - FM 11
     - ☐☐☐ Standard pattern
     - ☐☐☐ Nonstandard pattern
   - ☐☐☐ Additional items at CFI's discretion _____

   _____

5. Postflight critique and preview of next lesson

Completion Standards

The lesson will have been successfully completed when the pilot can demonstrate an understanding of localizer holding procedures. Additionally, the pilot will demonstrate greater proficiency in holding pattern entry procedures and VOR and GPS holding procedures. The pilot will be able to maintain the desired altitude, ±100 ft.; airspeed, ±10 kt.; and heading, ±10°; and to track a selected course or radial.

Instructor's comments: _____

_____

Lesson assignment: _____

_____

Notes: _____

_____

_____

_____

_____

_____

_____

FLIGHT LESSON 17: DME AND INTERSECTION HOLDING

FSTD/ATD option

Objective

To introduce the pilot to DME holding and intersection holding procedures. Additionally, the pilot's proficiency in other holding procedures is increased through practice.

Text References

Instrument Pilot Flight Maneuvers and Practical Test Prep (FM)

Content

1. Flight Lesson 16 complete? Yes ____   Copy of lesson placed in pilot's folder? Yes ____
2. Preflight briefing
3. Review items
   - ☐☐☐ ATC holding instructions
   - ☐☐☐ Holding pattern entry procedures
   - ☐☐☐ VOR holding procedures
   - ☐☐☐ GPS holding procedures
   - ☐☐☐ Localizer holding procedures
   - ☐☐☐ Use of autopilot for holding (if equipped)
   _____

4. New items
   - ☐☐☐ DME holding procedures - FM 11
     - ☐☐☐ Holding course away from the VORTAC or VOR/DME
     - ☐☐☐ Holding course toward the VORTAC or VOR/DME
   - ☐☐☐ Intersection holding - FM 11
     - ☐☐☐ Intersection defined by two VOR radials
   - ☐☐☐ Additional items at CFI's discretion _____
   _____

5. Postflight critique and preview of next lesson

Completion Standards

This lesson will have been successfully completed when the pilot can demonstrate an understanding of DME holding and intersection holding. Additionally, the pilot will demonstrate increased proficiency in VOR, GPS, and localizer holding procedures. The pilot will be able to maintain the desired altitude, ±100 ft.; airspeed, ±10 kt.; and heading, ±10°; and to track the desired radial or course.

Instructor's comments: _____

_____

Lesson assignment: _____

_____

Notes: _____

_____

_____

_____

_____

_____

_____

_____

FLIGHT LESSON 18: VOR INSTRUMENT APPROACH

FSTD/ATD option

Objective

To introduce the pilot to VOR instrument approach procedures, including ATC clearances that pertain to the approach. Additionally, the pilot will be able to properly enter the holding pattern depicted for the approach(es).

Text References

Instrument Pilot Flight Maneuvers and Practical Test Prep (FM)

Content

1. Flight Lesson 17 complete? Yes ____   Copy of lesson placed in pilot's folder? Yes ____
2. Preflight briefing
3. Review item
   ☐☐☐ Holding procedures
   _____

4. New items
   ☐☐☐ Segments of an instrument approach - FM Sec VI Intro
   ☐☐☐ Instrument approach procedure charts - FM Sec VI Intro
   ☐☐☐ Airplane approach category - FM Sec VI Intro
   ☐☐☐ Procedure turn - FM Sec VI Intro
   ☐☐☐ Advance information on instrument approach - FM Sec VI Intro
   ☐☐☐ Full approach - CFII
   ☐☐☐ Radar vectoring - FM Sec VI Intro
   ☐☐☐ ATC approach clearances - FM Sec VI Intro
   ☐☐☐ Inoperative airplane and ground navigation equipment - FM 16
   ☐☐☐ Inoperative visual aids associated with the landing environment - FM 16
   ☐☐☐ VOR, VOR/DME, VORTAC instrument approach procedures (full approach) - FM 16
        ☐☐☐ DME arc - FM 14
   ☐☐☐ Missed approach - FM 18
   ☐☐☐ Circling approach - FM 19
   ☐☐☐ Landing from an instrument approach - FM 20
   ☐☐☐ Additional items at CFI's discretion _____
   _____

5. Postflight critique and preview of next lesson

Completion Standards

The lesson will have been successfully completed when the pilot can explain and use the information on the approach charts, understand and comply with ATC approach clearances, and execute the approach and missed approach procedures. The pilot will be able to maintain altitude, ±100 ft.; airspeed, ±10 kt.; and heading, ±10°, with no more than a 3/4-scale deflection of the CDI, or within 10° in the case of an RMI, throughout the approach. Additionally, the pilot will demonstrate the proper holding pattern entry procedure and proper timing criteria or leg lengths, as appropriate.

Instructor's comments: _____

_____

Lesson assignment: _____

_____

Notes: _____

_____

_____

_____

FLIGHT LESSON 19: GPS INSTRUMENT APPROACHES

FSTD/ATD option

Objective

To introduce the pilot to GPS approach procedures. Additionally, the pilot will increase proficiency in VOR approach procedures.

Text References

Instrument Pilot Flight Maneuvers and Practical Test Prep (FM)

Content

1. Flight Lesson 18 complete? Yes ___   Copy of lesson placed in pilot's folder? Yes ___
2. Preflight briefing
3. Review items
   - ☐☐☐ Segments of an instrument approach
   - ☐☐☐ ATC approach clearances
   - ☐☐☐ Holding procedures
   - ☐☐☐ VOR instrument approach
   - ☐☐☐ Circling approach
   - ☐☐☐ Missed approach
   - ☐☐☐ Landing from an instrument approach
   - ☐☐☐ Automation management
     _____

4. New items
   - ☐☐☐ GPS receiver autonomous integrity monitoring (RAIM) - FM 8
   - ☐☐☐ GPS instrument approach design concepts - FM 16
   - ☐☐☐ GPS instrument approach procedures - FM 16
     - ☐☐☐ WAAS approach (if equipped and available)
     - ☐☐☐ Full approach
     - ☐☐☐ Radar vectors
     - ☐☐☐ Missed approach
   - ☐☐☐ Additional items at CFI's discretion _____
     _____

5. Postflight critique and preview of next lesson

Completion Standards

The lesson will have been successfully completed when the pilot can demonstrate the proper GPS approach and the missed approach procedures. The pilot will demonstrate an increased proficiency in holding, VOR approaches, circling approach procedures, and landing from an instrument approach. The pilot will be able to maintain the desired altitude, ±100 ft.; airspeed, ±10 kt.; heading, ±10°; and to maintain the GPS course (including vertical guidance if WAAS-equipped) with no more than a 3/4-scale deflection of the CDI.

Instructor's comments: _____

_____

Lesson assignment: _____

_____

Notes: _____

_____

_____

_____

FLIGHT LESSON 20: LOCALIZER INSTRUMENT APPROACH

FSTD/ATD option

Objective

To introduce the pilot to localizer instrument approach procedures. Additionally, the pilot will increase proficiency in VOR and GPS approaches.

Text References

Instrument Pilot Flight Maneuvers and Practical Test Prep (FM)

Content

1. Flight Lesson 19 complete? Yes ____   Copy of lesson placed in pilot's folder? Yes ___
2. Preflight briefing
3. Review items
    ☐☐☐ VOR instrument approach (partial panel)
    ☐☐☐ GPS instrument approach
    ☐☐☐ Missed approach
    ☐☐☐ Circling approach
    ☐☐☐ Landing from an instrument approach
    ☐☐☐ Recovery from unusual flight attitudes (without attitude indicator)
    ☐☐☐ Use of autopilot for holding (if equipped)
    _____

4. New items
    ☐☐☐ Localizer instrument approach - FM 16
            ☐☐☐ Missed approach
    ☐☐☐ Additional items at CFI's discretion _____

    _____

5. Postflight critique and preview of next lesson

Completion Standards

The lesson will have been successfully completed when the pilot can demonstrate knowledge in localizer instrument approach procedures. The pilot will be able to maintain the desired airspeed, ±10 kt.; heading, ±10°; and GPS CDI with no more than a 3/4-scale deflection. Prior to beginning the final approach segment, the pilot will maintain altitude, ±100 ft., and, while on the final approach segment, descend and maintain the MDA, +100/–50 ft. Additionally, the pilot will display proficiency in recovery from unusual flight attitudes.

Instructor's comments: _____

_____

Lesson assignment: _____

_____

Notes: _____

_____

_____

_____

_____

_____

_____

_____

_____

FLIGHT LESSON 21: ILS INSTRUMENT APPROACH

FSTD/ATD option

Objective

To introduce the pilot to the ILS instrument approach procedures. Additionally, the pilot will increase proficiency in GPS and localizer instrument approaches using full and partial panel.

Text References

Instrument Pilot Flight Maneuvers and Practical Test Prep (FM)
Pilot's Operating Handbook (POH)

Content

1. Flight Lesson 20 complete? Yes ____   Copy of lesson placed in pilot's folder? Yes ___
2. Preflight briefing
3. Review items
    - ☐☐☐ GPS instrument approach (partial panel)
    - ☐☐☐ Localizer instrument approach
    - ☐☐☐ Recovery from unusual flight attitudes (without attitude indicator)
    _____

4. New items
    - ☐☐☐ ILS instrument approach - FM 17
        - ☐☐☐ Missed approach - FM 18
        - ☐☐☐ Circling approach - FM 19
        - ☐☐☐ Use of autopilot during approach (if equipped) - POH 9
    - ☐☐☐ Proper autopilot management procedures (if equipped) - FM App A; POH 9
    - ☐☐☐ Additional items at CFI's discretion _____
    _____

5. Postflight critique and preview of next lesson

Completion Standards

The lesson will have been successfully completed when the pilot can demonstrate knowledge in ILS instrument approach procedures. The pilot will display an increase in proficiency in conducting GPS and localizer instrument approaches, including partial-panel approaches. During the nonprecision approaches, the pilot will be able to

1. Maintain, prior to the beginning of the final approach segment, altitude, ±100 ft.; heading, ±10°; and airspeed, ±10 kt.; with less than a full-scale deflection of the CDI or within 10° in the case of an RMI.
2. Arrive at the MDA prior to reaching the MAP.
3. Maintain, while on the final approach segment, no more than a 3/4-scale deflection of the CDI or within 10° in the case of an RMI; airspeed, ±10 kt.; and altitude, +100/–50 ft.

Additionally, the pilot will display proficiency in recovery from unusual flight attitudes.

Instructor's comments: _____

_____

Lesson assignment: _____

_____

Notes: _____

_____

_____

_____

FLIGHT LESSON 22: INSTRUMENT APPROACHES (REVIEW)

FSTD/ATD option

Objective

To review previous lessons to gain proficiency in instrument approaches (full and partial panel). Additionally, the pilot will be introduced to radar approaches (if available).

Text References

Instrument Pilot Flight Maneuvers and Practical Test Prep (FM)

Content

1. Flight Lesson 21 complete? Yes ___   Copy of lesson placed in pilot's folder? Yes ___
2. Preflight briefing
3. Review items
   ☐☐☐ VOR instrument approach
       ☐☐☐ Full panel
       ☐☐☐ Partial panel
   ☐☐☐ GPS instrument approach (precision and nonprecision)
       ☐☐☐ Full panel
       ☐☐☐ Partial panel
   ☐☐☐ Localizer instrument approach
       ☐☐☐ Full panel
       ☐☐☐ Partial panel
   ☐☐☐ ILS instrument approach (if available)
       ☐☐☐ Full panel
       ☐☐☐ Partial panel
       ☐☐☐ Circling approach
   ☐☐☐ Proper autopilot management procedures (if equipped) _____

4. New items
   ☐☐☐ Radar approaches (if available) - FM Sec VI Intro
       ☐☐☐ Precision approach (PAR)
       ☐☐☐ Surveillance approach (ASR)
       ☐☐☐ No-gyro approach (partial panel)
   ☐☐☐ Side-step maneuver - FM Sec VI Intro
   ☐☐☐ Additional items at CFI's discretion _____
   _____

5. Postflight critique and preview of next lesson

Completion Standards

The lesson will have been successfully completed when the pilot demonstrates an understanding of radar approaches and the side-step maneuver. Additionally, the pilot will demonstrate an increased proficiency in performing instrument approaches under both full- and partial-panel operations.

Instructor's comments: _____

_____

Lesson assignment: _____

_____

Notes: _____

_____

_____

FLIGHT LESSON 23: STAGE TWO CHECK

Objective

During this stage check, an authorized instructor will determine if the pilot is proficient in holding procedures and instrument approach procedures.

Content

1. Flight Lesson 22 complete? Yes ____   Copy of lesson placed in pilot's folder? Yes ____
2. Preflight briefing
3. Stage check tasks
   ☐☐☐ Holding procedures using navigation equipment in airplane
   ☐☐☐ ATC instructions and clearances relating to holding and approaches
   ☐☐☐ Nonprecision approaches (instructor to select at least one to conduct under partial panel)
      ☐☐☐ VOR approach
      ☐☐☐ GPS approach
      ☐☐☐ Localizer approach
   ☐☐☐ Precision approach
   ☐☐☐ Circling approach
   ☐☐☐ Missed approach
   ☐☐☐ Landing from an instrument approach   *DME ARC*
   ☐☐☐ Additional items at CFI's discretion _____

   _____

4. Postflight critique and preview of next lesson

Completion Standards

The lesson will have been successfully completed when the pilot can demonstrate proficiency in holding procedures and instrument approach procedures to the standards listed in the current FAA Instrument Rating Airman Certification Standards.

Instructor's comments: _____

_____

Lesson assignment: _____

_____

Notes: _____

_____

_____

_____

_____

_____

_____

_____

_____

_____

_____

_____

_____

_____

STAGE THREE

Stage Three Objective

The pilot will receive instruction in the proper procedures for cross-country flights in an airplane while operating under IFR within the U.S. National Airspace System. Additionally, the pilot will be instructed in the procedures to be used in the event of loss of communications. Finally, the pilot will receive instruction in preparation for the instrument rating (airplane) practical test.

Stage Three Completion Standards

The stage will be completed when the pilot demonstrates the ability to conduct cross-country flights in an airplane while operating under IFR, including the loss of communications procedures. Finally, the pilot will demonstrate proficiency in all tasks of the instrument rating (airplane) practical test and meet or exceed the minimum acceptable Airman Certification Standards for the instrument rating.

Lesson	Topic
	Stage Three
24	Cross-Country and Emergency Procedures
25	Cross-Country Procedures
26	Cross-Country Procedures
27	Maneuvers Review
28	Stage Three Check
29	End-of-Course Test

FLIGHT LESSON 24: CROSS-COUNTRY AND EMERGENCY PROCEDURES

FSTD/ATD option

Objective

To introduce the pilot to IFR cross-country procedures that include flight planning. Additionally, the pilot will be introduced to departure, en route, arrival, and loss of communications procedures.

Text References

Instrument Pilot Flight Maneuvers and Practical Test Prep (FM)
Pilot's Operating Handbook (POH)

Content

1. Flight Lesson 23 complete? Yes ___   Copy of lesson placed in pilot's folder? Yes ___
2. Preflight briefing
3. Review items
   - ☐☐☐ Airplane systems related to IFR operations
   - ☐☐☐ Airplane flight instruments and navigation equipment
   - ☐☐☐ Instrument flight deck check
   - ☐☐☐ Instrument takeoff
   - ☐☐☐ Intercepting and tracking navigational systems and DME arcs
   - ☐☐☐ Holding procedures
   - ☐☐☐ Arrival procedures
   - ☐☐☐ Instrument approach procedures
   - ☐☐☐ Loss of primary flight instrument indicators
   - ☐☐☐ Postflight procedures

4. New items
   - ☐☐☐ Preflight preparation - FM 4-6
   - ☐☐☐ Pilot qualifications - FM 4
   - ☐☐☐ Weather information - FM 5
   - ☐☐☐ Cross-country flight planning - FM 6
   - ☐☐☐ Air traffic control clearances - FM 10
   - ☐☐☐ Departure, en route, and arrival operations - FM 15
   - ☐☐☐ Emergency operations
     - ☐☐☐ Loss of communications - FM 21
     - ☐☐☐ Instrument, system, and equipment failures - POH 3, 9
     - ☐☐☐ Turbulence - FM 5; POH 3
     - ☐☐☐ Icing awareness, recognition, correction, and prevention - FM 5-7
     - ☐☐☐ Engine failure - POH 3
     - ☐☐☐ Low fuel status - CFII, POH 3
   - ☐☐☐ Calculating ETEs and ETAs - CFII
   - ☐☐☐ En route course changes - CFII
   - ☐☐☐ Additional items at CFI's discretion _____

5. Postflight critique and preview of next lesson

Completion Standards

The lesson will have been successfully completed when the pilot demonstrates an understanding of IFR flight planning; copying, readback, and compliance with ATC clearances; IFR departures and arrivals; and emergency operations. Additionally, the pilot will be able to calculate ETEs and ETAs and understand the reasons for course changes that are issued by ATC or requested due to weather conditions. The pilot will be able to maintain the desired altitude, ±100 ft.; airspeed, ±10 kt.; and heading, ±10°; and to track a course or radial.

Instructor's comments: _____

Lesson assignment: _____

Notes: _____

FLIGHT LESSON 25: CROSS-COUNTRY PROCEDURES

Objective

To increase the pilot's ability to conduct IFR cross-country operations. This flight should include an airport that is at least a straight-line distance of more than 50 NM from the departure point and, if possible, an airport that has a radar approach.

Content

1. Flight Lesson 24 complete? Yes ___   Copy of lesson placed in pilot's folder? Yes ___
2. Preflight briefing
3. Review items
   ☐☐☐ Weather information
   ☐☐☐ Cross-country flight planning
   ☐☐☐ Departure, en route, and arrival operations
   ☐☐☐ Holding procedures
   ☐☐☐ Instrument approach procedures
      ☐☐☐ Partial-panel nonprecision approach
      ☐☐☐ Missed approach
      ☐☐☐ Circling approach
      ☐☐☐ Radar or no-gyro approach (if available)
   ☐☐☐ Emergency operations
      ☐☐☐ Loss of communications
      ☐☐☐ Loss of primary flight instrument indicators
   ☐☐☐ Additional items at CFI's discretion _____

   _____

4. Postflight critique and preview of next lesson

Completion Standards

The lesson will have been successfully completed when the pilot demonstrates an increased proficiency in IFR flight planning, understanding and complying with ATC clearances, and conducting a cross-country flight under IFR. The pilot will be able to maintain the desired altitude, ±100 ft.; airspeed, ±10 kt.; and heading, ±10°; and to track a course or radial.

Instructor's comments: _____

_____

Lesson assignment: _____

_____

Notes: _____

_____

_____

_____

_____

_____

_____

_____

_____

_____

_____

_____

_____

FLIGHT LESSON 26: CROSS-COUNTRY PROCEDURES

Objective

To increase the pilot's proficiency in IFR cross-country operations. This cross-country flight must be performed under IFR and must be at least 250 NM along airways or ATC-directed routing with one segment of the flight consisting of at least a straight-line distance of 100 NM between airports. Additionally, it must involve an instrument approach at each airport and three different kinds of approaches with the use of navigation systems.

Content

1. Flight Lesson 25 complete? Yes ___   Copy of lesson placed in pilot's folder? Yes ___
2. Preflight briefing
3. Review items
   ☐☐☐ Weather information
   ☐☐☐ Cross-country flight planning
   ☐☐☐ Instrument takeoff
   ☐☐☐ Compliance with ATC clearances
   ☐☐☐ Holding procedures
   ☐☐☐ Precision approach
   ☐☐☐ Nonprecision approach (at least two different kinds of approaches)
   ☐☐☐ Missed approach
   ☐☐☐ Landing from an instrument approach
   ☐☐☐ Emergency operations (simulate)
      ☐☐☐ Loss of communications
      ☐☐☐ Loss of primary flight instrument indicators
      ☐☐☐ Low fuel supply
      ☐☐☐ Engine failure
   ☐☐☐ Additional items at CFI's discretion _____

   _____

4. Postflight critique and preview of next lesson

Completion Standards

The lesson will have been successfully completed when the pilot demonstrates a thorough understanding of IFR procedures. The pilot will complete each task to the standards specified in the current FAA Instrument Rating Airman Certification Standards.

Instructor's comments: _____

_____

Lesson assignment: _____

_____

Notes: _____

FLIGHT LESSON 27: MANEUVERS REVIEW

FSTD/ATD option

Objective

To review procedures and maneuvers covered previously.

Content

1. Flight Lesson 26 complete? Yes ___   Copy of lesson placed in pilot's folder? Yes ___
2. Preflight briefing
3. Review items
   - ☐☐☐ Airplane systems related to IFR operations
   - ☐☐☐ Airplane flight instruments and navigation equipment
   - ☐☐☐ Timed turns to magnetic compass headings
   - ☐☐☐ Steep turns
   - ☐☐☐ Recovery from unusual flight attitudes (without attitude indicator)
   - ☐☐☐ Additional items at CFI's discretion _____

   _____

4. Postflight critique and preview of next lesson

Completion Standards

The lesson will have been successfully completed when the pilot demonstrates proficiency in the maneuvers performed. The pilot will complete each task to the standards specified in the current FAA Instrument Rating Airman Certification Standards.

Instructor's comments: _____

_____

Lesson assignment:_____

_____

Notes: _____

_____

_____

_____

_____

_____

_____

_____

_____

_____

_____

_____

_____

_____

_____

_____

FLIGHT LESSON 28: STAGE THREE CHECK

Objective

During this stage check, an authorized instructor will determine if the student is proficient in IFR cross-country navigation.

Content

1. Flight Lesson 27 complete? Yes ___   Copy of lesson placed in pilot's folder? Yes ___
2. Preflight briefing
3. Stage check tasks
   ☐☐☐ Weather information
   ☐☐☐ Cross-country flight planning
   ☐☐☐ Air traffic control clearances
   ☐☐☐ Departure, en route, and arrival operations
   ☐☐☐ Holding procedures
   ☐☐☐ Straight-and-level flight
   ☐☐☐ Change of airspeed
   ☐☐☐ Constant airspeed climbs and descents
   ☐☐☐ Rate climbs and descents
   ☐☐☐ Timed turns to magnetic compass headings
   ☐☐☐ Recovery from unusual flight attitudes
   ☐☐☐ Intercepting and tracking navigational systems and DME arcs
   ☐☐☐ Loss of communications
   ☐☐☐ Loss of primary flight instrument indicators
   ☐☐☐ Checking instruments and equipment
   ☐☐☐ Instrument approach(es) at CFI's discretion _____
   _____

   ☐☐☐ Additional items at CFI's discretion _____
   _____

4. Postflight critique
5. Flight Lesson 28 complete? Yes ___

Completion Standards

The lesson will have been successfully completed when the pilot demonstrates the required level of proficiency in all stage check tasks based on the current FAA Instrument Rating Airman Certification Standards. If additional instruction is necessary, the flight instructor will assign the additional training. If the flight is satisfactory, the instructor will complete the pilot's training records and recommend the student for the End-of-Course Test.

Instructor's comments: _____

_____

Lesson assignment: _____

_____

Notes: _____

_____

_____

_____

_____

_____

_____

_____

FLIGHT LESSON 29: END-OF-COURSE TEST

Objective

The pilot will be able to demonstrate the required proficiency of an instrument-rated pilot by using the current FAA Instrument Rating Airman Certification Standards.

Content

1. Flight Lesson 28 complete? Yes ____   Copy of lesson placed in pilot's folder? Yes ____
2. Preflight briefing
3. Stage check tasks
   - ☐☐☐ Weather information
   - ☐☐☐ Cross-country flight planning
   - ☐☐☐ Airplane systems related to IFR operations
   - ☐☐☐ Airplane flight instruments and navigation equipment
   - ☐☐☐ Instrument and equipment flight deck check
   - ☐☐☐ Air traffic control clearances and procedures
   - ☐☐☐ Departure, en route, and arrival operations
   - ☐☐☐ Holding procedures
   - ☐☐☐ Straight-and-level flight
   - ☐☐☐ Change of airspeed
   - ☐☐☐ Constant airspeed climbs and descents
   - ☐☐☐ Rate climbs and descents
   - ☐☐☐ Timed turns to magnetic compass headings
   - ☐☐☐ Steep turns
   - ☐☐☐ Recovery from unusual flight attitudes
   - ☐☐☐ Intercepting and tracking navigational systems and DME arcs
   - ☐☐☐ Nonprecision approach (perform two, one using partial panel)
   - ☐☐☐ Precision approach
   - ☐☐☐ Missed approach
   - ☐☐☐ Circling approach
   - ☐☐☐ Landing from an instrument approach
   - ☐☐☐ Loss of communications
   - ☐☐☐ Loss of primary flight instrument indicators
   - ☐☐☐ Checking instruments and equipment
   - ☐☐☐ Automation management
   - ☐☐☐ Additional items at CFI's discretion _____
   _____

4. Postflight critique
5. Flight Lesson 29 complete? Yes ____
   Copy of lesson and graduation certificate placed in pilot's folder? Yes ____

Completion Standards

The lesson will have been successfully completed when the pilot demonstrates the required level of proficiency in all tasks of the current FAA Instrument Rating Airman Certification Standards. If additional instruction is necessary, the chief flight instructor will assign the additional training. If the flight is satisfactory, the chief instructor will complete the pilot's training records and issue a graduation certificate.

Instructor's comments: _____

_____

Lesson assignment: _____

_____

Notes: _____

_____

_____

_____

APPENDIX A
KNOWLEDGE TESTS AND FIGURES

For a copy of the answer key to all *Instrument Pilot Syllabus* Stage Tests, please email a request for the IPSYL Stage Test Answer Key to the Gleim Aviation Department at aviationteam@gleim.com.

STAGE ONE KNOWLEDGE TEST

1. (Refer to Figure 95 on page 93.) Which OBS selection on the No. 2 NAV would center the CDI and change the ambiguity indication to a TO?

A — 166°.
B — 346°.
C — 354°.

2. (Refer to Figure 109 on page 96.) In which general direction from the VORTAC is the aircraft located?

A — Northeast.
B — Southeast.
C — Southwest.

3. (Refer to Figure 98 on page 95 and Figure 99 on page 96.) To which aircraft position does HSI presentation "F" correspond?

A — 10
B — 14
C — 16

4. (Refer to Figure 147 on page 98.) Which is the correct sequence for recovery from the unusual attitude indicated?

A — Level wings, add power, lower nose, descend to original attitude, and heading.
B — Add power, lower nose, level wings, return to original attitude and heading.
C — Stop turn by raising right wing and add power at the same time, lower the nose, and return to original attitude and heading.

5. Which practical test should be made on the electric gyro instruments prior to starting an engine?

A — Check that the electrical connections are secure on the back of the instruments.
B — Check that the attitude of the miniature aircraft is wings level before turning on electrical power.
C — Turn on the electrical power and listen for any unusual or irregular mechanical noise.

6. To level off at an airspeed higher than the descent speed, the addition of power should be made, assuming a 500 FPM rate of descent, at approximately

A — 50 to 100 feet above the desired altitude.
B — 100 to 150 feet above the desired altitude.
C — 150 to 200 feet above the desired altitude.

7. Your transponder is inoperative. What are the requirements for flying in Class D airspace?

A — The entry into Class D is prohibited.
B — Continue the flight as planned.
C — Pilot must immediately request priority handling to proceed to destination.

8. Which of the following is a benefit of flying with an autopilot?

A — Pilots will not need to worry about controlling airspeed or throttle settings.
B — Airspace restrictions will automatically be avoided.
C — Pilot workload is reduced.

9. When airspeed is increased in a turn, what must be done to maintain a constant altitude?

A — Decrease the angle of bank.
B — Increase the angle of bank and/or decrease the angle of attack.
C — Decrease the angle of attack.

10. While cruising at 190 knots, you wish to establish a climb at 160 knots. When entering the climb (full panel), it would be proper to make the initial pitch change by increasing back elevator pressure until the

A — attitude indicator shows the approximate pitch attitude appropriate for the 160-knot climb.
B — attitude indicator, airspeed, and vertical speed indicate a climb.
C — airspeed indication reaches 160 knots.

11. What should be the indication on the magnetic compass as you roll into a standard-rate turn to the left from an east heading in the Northern Hemisphere?

A — The compass will initially indicate a turn to the right.
B — The compass will remain on east for a short time, then gradually catch up to the magnetic heading of the aircraft.
C — The compass will indicate the approximate correct magnetic heading if the roll into the turn is smooth.

12. The primary reason the pitch attitude must be increased, to maintain a constant altitude during a coordinated turn, is because the

A — thrust is acting in a different direction, causing a reduction in airspeed and loss of lift.
B — vertical component of lift has decreased as the result of the bank.
C — use of pedals has increased the drag.

13. (Refer to Figure 82 on page 89.) Which is an acceptable range of accuracy when performing an operational check of dual VOR's using one system against the other?

A — 1
B — 2
C — 4

14. The local altimeter setting should be used by all pilots in a particular area, primarily to provide for

A — the cancellation of altimeter error due to nonstandard temperatures aloft.
B — better vertical separation of aircraft.
C — more accurate terrain clearance in mountainous areas.

15. During IFR en route operations using an approved TSO-C129 or TSO-C196 GPS system for navigation,

A — no other navigation system is required.
B — active monitoring of an alternate navigation system is always required.
C — the aircraft must have an approved TSO-C129 or TSO-C196 and operational alternate navigation system appropriate for the route.

16. Which checks and inspections of flight instruments or instrument systems must be accomplished before an aircraft can be flown under IFR?

A — VOR within 30 days, altimeter systems within 24 calendar months, and transponder within 24 calendar months.
B — ELT test within 30 days, altimeter systems within 12 calendar months, and transponder within 24 calendar months.
C — VOR within 24 calendar months, transponder within 24 calendar months, and altimeter system within 12 calendar months.

17. After your recent IFR experience lapses, how much time do you have before you must pass an instrument proficiency check to act as pilot in command under IFR?

A — 6 months.
B — 90 days.
C — 12 months.

18. To meet the minimum instrument experience requirements, within the last 6 calendar months you need

A — six instrument approaches, holding procedures, and intercepting and tracking courses in the appropriate category of aircraft.
B — six hours in the same category aircraft.
C — six hours in the same category aircraft, and at least 3 of the 6 hours in actual IFR conditions.

19. An instrument rated pilot who has not logged any instrument time in 1 year or more cannot serve as pilot in command under IFR, unless the pilot

A — completes the required 6 hours and six approaches, followed by an instrument proficiency check given by an FAA-designated examiner.
B — passes an instrument proficiency check in the category of aircraft involved, given by an approved FAA examiner, instrument instructor, or FAA inspector.
C — passes an instrument proficiency check in the category of aircraft involved, followed by 6 hours and six instrument approaches, 3 of those hours in the category of aircraft involved.

20. A certificated commercial pilot who carries passengers for hire at night or in excess of 50 NM is required to have at least

A — a type rating.
B — a first-class medical certificate.
C — an instrument rating in the same category and class of aircraft.

STAGE TWO KNOWLEDGE TEST

1. What does the ATC term "Radar Contact" signify?

A — Your aircraft has been identified and you will receive separation from all aircraft while in contact with this radar facility.

B — Your aircraft has been identified on the radar display and radar flight-following will be provided until radar identification is terminated.

C — You will be given traffic advisories until advised the service has been terminated or that radar contact has been lost.

2. (Refer to Figure 230 on page 105 and Figure 231 on page 106.) You plan to fly to Baldwin for Christmas. What minimum equipment is required for the VOR/DME or GPS-A procedure, and can you complete the flight?

A — One VOR receiver; yes, the trip will be fun.

B — One VOR receiver and one DME receiver; no flight though, the airport is closed.

C — Two VOR receivers; yes, but no fuel is available because the airport is unattended.

3. (Refer to Figure 175 on page 101 and Figure 174 on page 100.) At which point does the JEN.JEN9 arrival begin?

A — INK VOR.

B — GLEN ROSE VORTAC.

C — FEVER intersection.

4. (Refer to Figure 217 on page 104.) The symbol on the plan view of the ILS or LOC RWY 13 procedure at DSM represents a minimum safe sector altitude within 25 NM of

A — Des Moines VORTAC.

B — CLIVE outer marker.

C — Des Moines International Airport.

5. (Refer to Figure 234 on page 107.) What options are available concerning the teardrop course reversal for LOC RWY 18 approach to Lincoln?

A — If a course reversal is required, only the teardrop can be executed.

B — The point where the turn is begun and the type and rate of turn are optional.

C — A normal procedure turn may be made if the 10 DME limit is not exceeded.

6. (Refer to Figure 247 on page 109.) What is the minimum altitude descent procedure if cleared for the S-ILS 9 approach from Seal Beach VORTAC?

A — Descend and maintain 3,000 to JASER INT, descend to and maintain 2,500 until crossing EXPAM, descend to 1,280 (DA).

B — Descend and maintain 3,000 to JASER INT, descend to 2,800 when established on the LOC course, intercept and maintain the GS to 960 (DA).

C — Descend and maintain 3,000 to JASER INT, descend to 2,500 while established on the LOC course inbound, intercept and maintain the GS to 960 (DA).

7. (Refer to Figure 238 on page 108.) If cleared for the RNAV (GPS) RWY 28 approach (Lancaster/Fairfield) over APE VORTAC, what will ATC expect of you?

A — Proceed to CASER, use the S-28 LOC 1620-1 minimums.

B — Proceed straight in from FAIRF, descend after FAIRF.

C — Proceed direct to FAIRF and execute the parallel entry depicted on the instrument approach procedure.

8. What effect does haze have on the ability to see traffic or terrain features during flight?

A — Haze causes the eyes to focus at infinity, making terrain features harder to see.

B — The eyes tend to overwork in haze and do not detect relative movement easily.

C — Haze creates the illusion of being a greater distance than actual from the runway, and causes pilots to fly a lower approach.

9. What is the purpose of the runway exit sign?

A — Defines direction and designation of runway when exiting a taxiway.

B — Defines direction and designation of exit taxiway from runway.

C — Defines a mandatory exit point from the runway during Land and Hold Short Operations (LAHSO).

10. When is radar service terminated during a visual approach?

A — Automatically when ATC instructs the pilot to contact the tower.

B — Immediately upon acceptance of the approach by the pilot.

C — When ATC advises, "Radar service terminated; resume own navigation."

11. Which information is always given in an abbreviated departure clearance?

A — DP or transition name and altitude to maintain.
B — Name of destination airport or specific fix and altitude.
C — Altitude to maintain and code to squawk.

12. During a flight, the controller advises "traffic 2 o'clock 5 miles southbound." The pilot is holding 20° correction for a crosswind from the right. Where should the pilot look for the traffic?

A — 40° to the right of the aircraft's nose.
B — 20° to the right of the aircraft's nose.
C — Straight ahead.

13. Why is fatigue hazardous to flight safety?

A — The pilot hurries to get done in order to rest.
B — Fatigue may not be apparent to a pilot until serious errors are made (an impaired pilot is a dangerous pilot).
C — The pilot is lazy and rushes to get done quickly.

14. A sloping cloud formation, an obscured horizon, and a dark scene spread with ground lights and stars can create an illusion known as

A — elevator illusions.
B — autokinesis.
C — false horizons.

15. What visual illusion creates the same effect as a narrower-than-usual runway?

A — An upsloping runway.
B — A wider-than-usual runway.
C — A downsloping runway.

16. Why is hypoxia particularly dangerous during flights with one pilot?

A — Night vision may be so impaired that the pilot cannot see other aircraft.
B — Symptoms of hypoxia may be difficult to recognize before the pilot's reactions are affected.
C — The pilot may not be able to control the aircraft even if using oxygen.

17. Which is not a type of hypoxia?

A — Histotoxic.
B — Hypoxic.
C — Hypertoxic.

18. A pilot is more subject to spatial disorientation if

A — kinesthetic senses are ignored.
B — eyes are moved often in the process of cross-checking the flight instruments.
C — body signals are used to interpret flight attitude.

19. What is meant when departure control instructs you to "resume own navigation" after you have been vectored to a Victor airway?

A — You should maintain the airway by use of your navigation equipment.
B — Radar service is terminated.
C — You are still in radar contact, but must make position reports.

20. What is the procedure when the DME malfunctions at or above 24,000 feet MSL?

A — Notify ATC immediately and request an altitude below 24,000 feet.
B — Continue to your destination in VFR conditions and report the malfunction.
C — After immediately notifying ATC, you may continue to the next airport of intended landing where repairs can be made.

STAGE THREE KNOWLEDGE TEST

1. (Refer to Figure 91 on page 92.) Southbound on V257, at what time should you arrive at DBS VORTAC if you crossed over CPN VORTAC at 0850 and over DIVID intersection at 0854?

A — 0939
B — 0943
C — 0947

2. (Refer to Figure 65 on page 87.) Which point would be the appropriate VOR COP on V552 from the LFT to the TBD VORTACs?

A — CLYNT intersection.
B — HATCH intersection.
C — 34 DME from the LFT VORTAC.

3. (Refer to Figure 89 on page 91.) What VHF frequencies are available for communications with Cedar City FSS?

A — 123.6, 121.5, 108.6, and 112.8.
B — 122.2, 121.5, 122.6, and 122.1.
C — 122.2, 121.5, 122.0, and 123.6.

4. (Refer to Figure 24 on page 85.) For planning purposes, what would be the highest MEA on V187 between Grand Junction, Walker Airport, and Durango, La Plata Co. Airport?

A — 12,000 feet.
B — 15,000 feet.
C — 16,000 feet.

5. The reporting station originating this Aviation Routine Weather Report has a field elevation of 620 feet. If the reported sky cover is one continuous layer, what is its thickness (tops of OVC are reported at 6,500 feet)?

METAR KMDW 121856Z AUTO 32005KT 1 1/2SM
  +RA BR OVC007 17/16 A2980

A — 5,180 feet.
B — 5,800 feet.
C — 5,880 feet.

6. Which response most closely interprets the following PIREP?

UA/OV OKC 063064/TM 1522/FL080/TP C172/TA –
  04 /WV245040/TB LGT/RM IN CLR.

A — 64 nautical miles on the 63 degree radial from Oklahoma City VOR at 1522 UTC, flight level 8,000 feet. Type of aircraft is a Cessna 172.
B — Reported by a Cessna 172, turbulence and light rime icing in climb to 8,000 ft.
C — 63 nautical miles on the 64 degree radial from Oklahoma City, thunderstorm and light rain at 1522 UTC.

7. (Refer to Figure 2 on page 84.) What approximate wind direction, speed, and temperature (relative to ISA) should a pilot expect when planning for a flight over ALB at FL 270?

A — 270° magnetic at 97 knots; ISA –4°C.
B — 260° true at 110 knots; ISA +5°C.
C — 275° true at 97 knots; ISA +4°C.

8. (Refer to Figure 175 on page 101 and Figure 174 on page 100.) When DFW is landing to the north, at CURLE, expect

A — to be instructed to maintain 200 knots.
B — to fly a course of 010°.
C — radar vectors.

9. With regards to icing, which is true?

A — Heavy icing on the leading edge is not as bad as light icing on the upper surface.
B — Smooth ice on the upper surface will not cause any problems.
C — Light icing is more of a problem than heavy icing.

10. (Refer to Figure 192 on page 102.) Using an average ground speed of 90 knots, what constant rate of descent from 3,100 feet MSL at the 6 DME fix would enable the aircraft to arrive at 2,400 feet MSL at the FAF?

A — 350 feet per minute.
B — 400 feet per minute.
C — 450 feet per minute.

11. A high cloud is composed mostly of

A — ozone.
B — condensation nuclei.
C — ice crystals.

12. Winds at 5,000 feet AGL on a particular flight are southwesterly while most of the surface winds are southerly. This difference in direction is primarily due to

A — a stronger pressure gradient at higher altitudes.
B — friction between the wind and the surface.
C — stronger Coriolis force at the surface.

13. (Refer to Figure 192 on page 102.) As a guide in making range corrections, how many degrees of relative bearing change should be used for each one-half-mile deviation from the desired arc?

A — 2° to 3°.
B — 5° maximum.
C — 10° to 20°.

14. Which conditions are favorable for the formation of radiation fog?

A — Moist air moving over colder ground or water.
B — Cloudy sky and a light wind moving saturated warm air over a cool surface.
C — Clear sky, little or no wind, small temperature/dew point spread, and over a land surface.

15. Test data indicates that ice, snow, or frost having a thickness and roughness similar to medium or coarse sandpaper on the leading edge and upper surface of an airfoil can

A — increase drag and reduce lift by as much as 40 percent.
B — reduce lift by as much as 40 percent and increase drag by 30 percent.
C — reduce lift by as much as 30 percent and increase drag by 40 percent.

16. On which surface of the aircraft could a pilot generally expect to see the first sign of ice accumulation?

A — Pitot tube.
B — Wing.
C — Propeller.

17. When is the wind group at one of the forecast altitudes omitted at a specific location or station in the Wind and Temperature Aloft Forecast (FB)? When the wind

A — is less than 5 knots.
B — is less than 10 knots.
C — at the altitude is within 1,500 feet of the station elevation.

18. When the visibility is greater than 6 SM on a TAF it is

A — expressed as 6PSM.
B — expressed as P6SM.
C — omitted from the report.

19. When operating under IFR with a VFR-On-Top clearance, what altitude should be maintained?

A — An IFR cruising altitude appropriate to the magnetic course being flown.
B — A VFR cruising altitude appropriate to the magnetic course being flown and as restricted by ATC.
C — The last IFR altitude assigned by ATC.

20. (Refer to Figure 31 on page 86.) What minimum navigation equipment is required en route on V448 to identify MOPIO?

A — One VOR receiver.
B — Two VOR receivers and DME.
C — One VOR receiver and DME.

END-OF-COURSE KNOWLEDGE TEST

1. If the outside air temperature increases during a flight at constant power and at a constant indicated altitude, the true airspeed will

A — decrease and true altitude will increase.
B — increase and true altitude will decrease.
C — increase and true altitude will increase.

2. A ceiling is defined as the height of the

A — highest layer of clouds or obscuring phenomena aloft that covers over 6/10 of the sky.
B — lowest layer of clouds that contributed to the overall overcast.
C — lowest layer of clouds or obscuring phenomena aloft that is reported as broken or overcast.

3. What relationship exists between the winds at 2,000 feet above the surface and the surface winds?

A — The winds at 2,000 feet and the surface winds flow in the same direction, but the surface winds are weaker due to friction.
B — The winds at 2,000 feet tend to parallel the isobars while the surface winds cross the isobars at an angle toward lower pressure and are weaker.
C — The surface winds tend to veer to the right of the winds at 2,000 feet and are usually weaker.

4. (Refer to Figure 140 on page 97, Figure 141 on page 97, and Figure 142 on page 97.) Which displacement from the localizer centerline and glide slope indicates you are high and to the left of the ILS course?

A — Figure 140.
B — Figure 141.
C — Figure 142.

5. (Refer to Figure 211 on page 103.) For takeoff on RWY 9 using an average groundspeed of 140 knots, what minimum rate of climb would meet the required minimum rate of climb as specified on the instrument departure procedure?

A — 830 feet per minute.
B — 415 feet per minute.
C — 970 feet per minute.

6. (Refer to Figure 165 on page 99.) Which restriction to the use of the OED VORTAC would be applicable to the (GNATS6.MOURN) departure?

A — R-295 beyond 35 NM below 8,500 feet.
B — R-210 beyond 35 NM below 8,500 feet.
C — R-265 within 15 NM below 9,000 feet.

7. (Refer to Figure 96 on page 93 and Figure 97 on page 94.) To which aircraft position(s) does HSI presentation "E" correspond?

A — 8 only.
B — 3 only.
C — 8 and 3.

8. (Refer to Figure 65 on page 87 and Figure 66 on page 88.) What is your position relative to GRICE intersection?

A — Right of V552 and approaching GRICE intersection.
B — Right of V552 and past GRICE intersection.
C — Left of V552 and approaching GRICE intersection.

9. (Refer to Figure 87 on page 90.) While holding at the 10 DME fix east of LCH for an ILS approach to RWY 15 at Lake Charles Muni Airport, ATC advises you to expect clearance for the approach at 1015. At 1000 you experience two-way radio communications failure. Which procedure should be followed?

A — Squawk 7600 and listen on the LOM frequency for instructions from ATC. If no instructions are received, start your approach at 1015.
B — Squawk 7700 for 1 minute, then 7600. After 1 minute, descend to the minimum final approach fix altitude. Start your approach at 1015.
C — Squawk 7600; plan to begin your approach at 1015.

10. (Refer to Figure 87 on page 90.) At STRUT intersection headed eastbound, ATC instructs you to hold west on the 10 DME fix west of LCH on V306, standard turns. What entry procedure is recommended?

A — Direct.
B — Teardrop.
C — Parallel.

11. (Refer to Figure 24 on page 85.) While passing near the CORTEZ VOR, southbound on V187, contact is lost with Denver Center. You should attempt to reestablish contact with Denver Center on

A — 118.575 MHz.
B — 108.4 MHz.
C — 122.3 MHz.

12. SIGMETs are issued as a warning of weather conditions potentially hazardous

A — particularly to large commercial operators.
B — to all aircraft regardless of size or operating environment.
C — particularly to light aircraft.

13. (Refer to Figure 2 on page 84.) What approximate wind direction, speed, and temperature (relative to ISA) should a pilot expect when planning for a flight over ALB at FL 270?

A — 270° magnetic at 97 knots; ISA –4°C.
B — 260° true at 110 knots; ISA +5°C.
C — 275° true at 97 knots; ISA +4°C.

14. (Refer to Figure 91 on page 92.) What are the oxygen requirements for an IFR flight eastbound on V520 from DBS VORTAC in an unpressurized aircraft at the MEA?

A — The required minimum crew must be provided and use supplemental oxygen for that part of the flight of more than 30 minutes.
B — The required minimum crew must be provided and use supplemental oxygen for that part of the flight of more than 30 minutes, and the passengers must be provided supplemental oxygen.
C — The required minimum crew must be provided and use supplemental oxygen, and the passengers must be provided supplemental oxygen.

15. (Refer to Figure 234 on page 107.) What options are available concerning the teardrop course reversal for LOC RWY 18 approach to Lincoln?

A — If a course reversal is required, only the teardrop can be executed.
B — The point where the turn is begun and the type and rate of turn are optional.
C — A normal procedure turn may be made if the 10 DME limit is not exceeded.

16. (Refer to Figure 65 on page 87 and Figure 67 on page 88.) What is the significance of the symbol at GRICE intersection?

A — It signifies a localizer-only approach is available at Harry P. Williams Memorial.
B — The localizer has an additional navigation function.
C — GRICE intersection also serves as the FAF for the ILS approach procedure to Harry P. Williams Memorial.

17. (Refer to Figure 174 on page 100 and Figure 175 on page 101.) On which heading should you plan to depart DELMO intersection?

A — 016°.
B — 039°.
C — 355°.

18. When ATC has not imposed any climb or descent restrictions and aircraft are within 1,000 feet of assigned altitude, pilots should attempt to both climb and descend at a rate of between

A — 500 feet per minute and 1,000 feet per minute.
B — 500 feet per minute and 1,500 feet per minute.
C — 1,000 feet per minute and 2,000 feet per minute.

19. The proper use of deicing boots should include

A — activation of the system at the first indication of icing and the continued cycling of the boots after leaving icing conditions to ensure any residual ice has been removed.
B — activation of the system at the first indication of icing and the one cycle of the boots after leaving icing conditions to ensure any residual ice has been removed.
C — discontinue the use of the boots upon exiting icing conditions.

20. What is the minimum flight visibility and distance from clouds for flight at 10,500 feet with a VFR-on-Top clearance during daylight hours? (Class E airspace.)

A — 3 SM, 1,000 feet above, 500 feet below, and 2,000 feet horizontal.
B — 5 SM, 1,000 feet above, 1,000 feet below, and 1 mile horizontal.
C — 5 SM, 1,000 feet above, 500 feet below, and 1 mile horizontal.

21. While on an IFR flight plan, you should notify ATC of a variation in speed when

A — ground speed changes more than 5 knots.
B — average TAS changes 10 knots or 5 percent.
C — ground speed changes 10 MPH or more.

22. Pilots of IFR flights seeking ATC in-flight weather avoidance assistance should keep in mind that

A — ATC radar limitations and, frequency congestion may limit the controllers capability to provide this service.
B — circumnavigating severe weather can only be accommodated in the en route areas away from terminals because of congestion.
C — ATC Narrow Band Radar does not provide the controller with weather intensity capability.

23. To level off from a descent to a specific altitude, the pilot should lead the level-off by approximately

A — 10 percent of the vertical speed.
B — 30 percent of the vertical speed.
C — 50 percent of the vertical speed.

24. In a left turn, correct control coordination is indicated by

A — The ball of the turn coordinator in the center.
B — The ball of the turn coordinator to the left of center.
C — The ball of the turn coordinator to the right of center.

25. The suffix "nimbus", used in naming clouds, means a

A — cloud with extensive vertical development.
B — rain cloud.
C — dark massive, towering cloud.

26. What action is recommended if a pilot does not wish to use an instrument departure procedure?

A — Advise clearance delivery or ground control before departure.
B — Advise departure control upon initial contact.
C — Enter "No DP" in the REMARKS section of the IFR flight plan.

27. What should be the indication on the magnetic compass as you roll into a standard-rate turn to the left from an east heading in the Northern Hemisphere?

A — The compass will initially indicate a turn to the right.
B — The compass will remain on east for a short time, then gradually catch up to the magnetic heading of the aircraft.
C — The compass will indicate the approximate correct magnetic heading if the roll into the turn is smooth.

28. Unless otherwise specified on the chart, the minimum en route altitude along a jet route is

A — 18,000 feet MSL.
B — 24,000 feet MSL.
C — 10,000 feet MSL.

29. When should pilots state their position on the airport when calling the tower for takeoff?

A — When visibility is less than 1 mile.
B — When parallel runways are in use.
C — When departing from a runway intersection.

30. (Refer to Figure 1A on page 83.) If more than one cruising altitude is intended, what information should be entered in item 15, "Level," of the flight plan?

A — Initial cruising altitude.
B — Highest cruising altitude.
C — Lowest cruising altitude.

31. (Refer to Figure 1A on page 83.) What information should be entered in item 19, "Endurance," for an IFR flight?

A — The estimated time en route plus 30 minutes.
B — The estimated time en route plus 45 minutes.
C — The amount of usable fuel on board expressed in time.

32. What types of surfaces are most likely to see the first signs of ice accumulation?

A — Large wide areas.
B — Small narrow areas.
C — Areas made from metal.

33. During normal flight with a vacuum driven attitude indicator, control pressures normally should not move the horizon bar more than

A — One bar width, with not more than an additional one bar width for normal flight deviations.
B — One-half bar width, with not more than an additional one bar width for normal flight deviations.
C — One-half bar width, with not more than an additional one-half bar width for normal flight deviations.

34. A prognostic chart depicts the conditions

A — existing at the surface during the past 6 hours.
B — which presently exist from the 1,000-millibar through the 700-millibar level.
C — forecast to exist at a specific time in the future.

35. Flying clear of clouds on an instrument flight plan, what are the requirements for a contact approach to an airport that has an approved IAP?

A — The controller must determine that the pilot can see the airport at the altitude flown and can remain clear of clouds.
B — The controller must have determined that the visibility was at least 1 mile and be reasonably sure the pilot can remain clear of clouds.
C — The pilot must request the approach, have at least 1 mile visibility, and be reasonably sure of remaining clear of clouds.

36. When making an instrument approach at the selected alternate airport, what landing minimums apply?

A — Standard alternate minimums (600-2 or 800-2).
B — The IFR alternate minimums listed for that airport.
C — The landing minimums published for the type of procedure selected.

37. What does the symbol T within a black triangle in the minimums section of the IAP for a particular airport indicate?

A — Takeoff minimums are 1 mile for aircraft having two engines or less and 1/2 mile for those with more than two engines.
B — Instrument takeoffs are not authorized.
C — Takeoff minimums are not standard and/or departure procedures are published.

38. What altitude may a pilot on an IFR flight plan select upon receiving a VFR-on-Top clearance?

A — Any altitude at least 1,000 feet above or 1,000 feet below the meteorological condition.
B — Any appropriate VFR altitude at or above the MEA in VFR weather conditions.
C — Any VFR altitude appropriate for the direction of flight at least 500 feet above the meteorological condition.

39. When on a VFR-on-Top clearance, the cruising altitude is based on

A — true course.
B — magnetic course.
C — magnetic heading.

40. When the CDI needle is centered during an airborne VOR check, the omni-bearing selector and the TO/FROM indicator should read

A — within 4° of the selected radial.
B — within 6° of the selected radial.
C — 0° TO, only if you are due south of the VOR.

41. (Refer to Figure 13 on page 84.) When penetrating a microburst, which aircraft will experience an increase in performance without a change in pitch or power?

A — 3.
B — 2.
C — 1.

42. Which is not a type of hypoxia?

A — Histotoxic.
B — Hypoxic.
C — Hypertoxic.

43. The sensations which lead to spatial disorientation during instrument flight conditions

A — are frequently encountered by beginning instrument pilots, but never by pilots with moderate instrument experience.
B — occur, in most instances, during the initial period of transition from visual to instrument flight.
C — must be suppressed and complete reliance placed on the indications of the flight instruments.

44. How can an instrument pilot best overcome spatial disorientation?

A — Rely on kinesthetic sense.
B — Use a very rapid cross-check.
C — Read and interpret the flight instruments, and act accordingly.

45. Pressure altitude is the altitude read on your altimeter when the instrument is adjusted to indicate height above

A — sea level.
B — the standard datum plane.
C — ground level.

46. During IFR en route and terminal operations using an approved TSO-C129 or TSO-C196 GPS system for navigation, ground based navigational facilities

A — are only required during the approach portion of the flight.
B — must be operational along the entire route.
C — must be operational only if RAIM predicts an outage.

47. Which procedure should you follow if you experience two-way communications failure while holding at a holding fix with an EFC time? (The holding fix is not the same as the approach fix.)

A — Depart the holding fix to arrive at the approach fix as close as possible to the EFC time.
B — Depart the holding fix at the EFC time.
C — Proceed immediately to the approach fix and hold until EFC.

48. To operate under IFR below 18,000 feet, a pilot must file an IFR flight plan and receive an appropriate ATC clearance prior to

A — entering controlled airspace.
B — entering weather conditions below VFR minimums.
C — takeoff.

49. When simultaneous approaches are in progress, how does each pilot receive radar advisories?

A — On tower frequency.
B — On approach control frequency.
C — One pilot on tower frequency and the other on approach control frequency.

50. A pilot may satisfy the recent flight experience requirement necessary to act as pilot in command in IMC in powered aircraft by logging within the 6 calendar months preceding the month of the flight

A — six instrument approaches, holding procedures, and intercepting and tracking courses using navigational systems.
B — six instrument approaches and 3 hours under actual or 6 hours in simulated IFR conditions; three of the approaches must be in the category of aircraft involved.
C — 6 hours of instrument time under actual or simulated IFR conditions, including at least six instrument approaches. Three of the 6 hours must be in flight in any category aircraft.

51. You check the flight instruments while taxiing and find the vertical speed indicator (VSI) indicates a descent of 100 feet per minute. In this case, you

A — may not proceed under IFR until the instrument is corrected by an authorized instrument repairman.
B — may take off under IFR and use 100 feet descent as the zero indication.
C — may take off and proceed under IFR but only in VFR weather conditions.

52. Which sources of aeronautical information, when used collectively, provide the latest status of airport conditions (e.g., runway closures, runway lighting, snow conditions)?

A — *Aeronautical Information Manual*, aeronautical charts, and Distant (D) NOTAMs.
B — Chart Supplement and FDC NOTAMs.
C — Chart Supplement and Distant (D) NOTAMs.

53. If squalls are reported at your destination, what wind conditions should you anticipate?

A — Sudden increases in wind speed of at least 16 knots rising to 22 knots or more, lasting for at least 1 minute.
B — Peak gusts of at least 35 knots for a sustained period of 1 minute or longer.
C — Rapid variation in wind direction of at least 20° and changes in speed of at least 10 knots between peaks and lulls.

54. During the life cycle of a thunderstorm, which stage is characterized predominantly by downdrafts?

A — Cumulus.
B — Dissipating.
C — Mature.

55. What indication should a pilot receive when a VOR station is undergoing maintenance and may be considered unreliable?

A — No coded identification, but possible navigation indications.
B — Coded identification, but no navigation indications.
C — A voice recording on the VOR frequency announcing that the VOR is out of service for maintenance.

56. When checking the sensitivity of a VOR receiver, the number of degrees in course change as the OBS is rotated to move the CDI from center to the last dot on either side should be between

A — 5° and 6°.
B — 8° and 10°.
C — 10° and 12°.

57. How should the pilot make a VOR receiver check when the aircraft is located on the designated checkpoint on the airport surface?

A — With the aircraft headed directly toward the VOR and the OBS set to 000°, the CDI should center within plus or minus 4° of that radial with a TO indication.
B — Set the OBS on the designated radial. The CDI must center within plus or minus 4° of that radial with a FROM indication.
C — Set the OBS on 180° plus or minus 4°; the CDI should center with a FROM indication.

58. What is the maximum tolerance allowed for an operational VOR equipment check when using a VOT?

A — Plus or minus 4°.
B — Plus or minus 6°.
C — Plus or minus 8°.

59. When must an operational check on the aircraft VOR equipment be accomplished when used to operate under IFR?

A — Within the preceding 10 days or 10 hours of flight time.
B — Within the preceding 30 days or 30 hours of flight time.
C — Within the preceding 30 days.

60. Frontal waves normally form on

A — slow moving cold fronts or stationary fronts.
B — slow moving warm fronts and strong occluded fronts.
C — rapidly moving cold fronts or warm fronts.

FIGURES FOR KNOWLEDGE TESTS

All FAA figures required for the knowledge tests are located below and on the following pages.

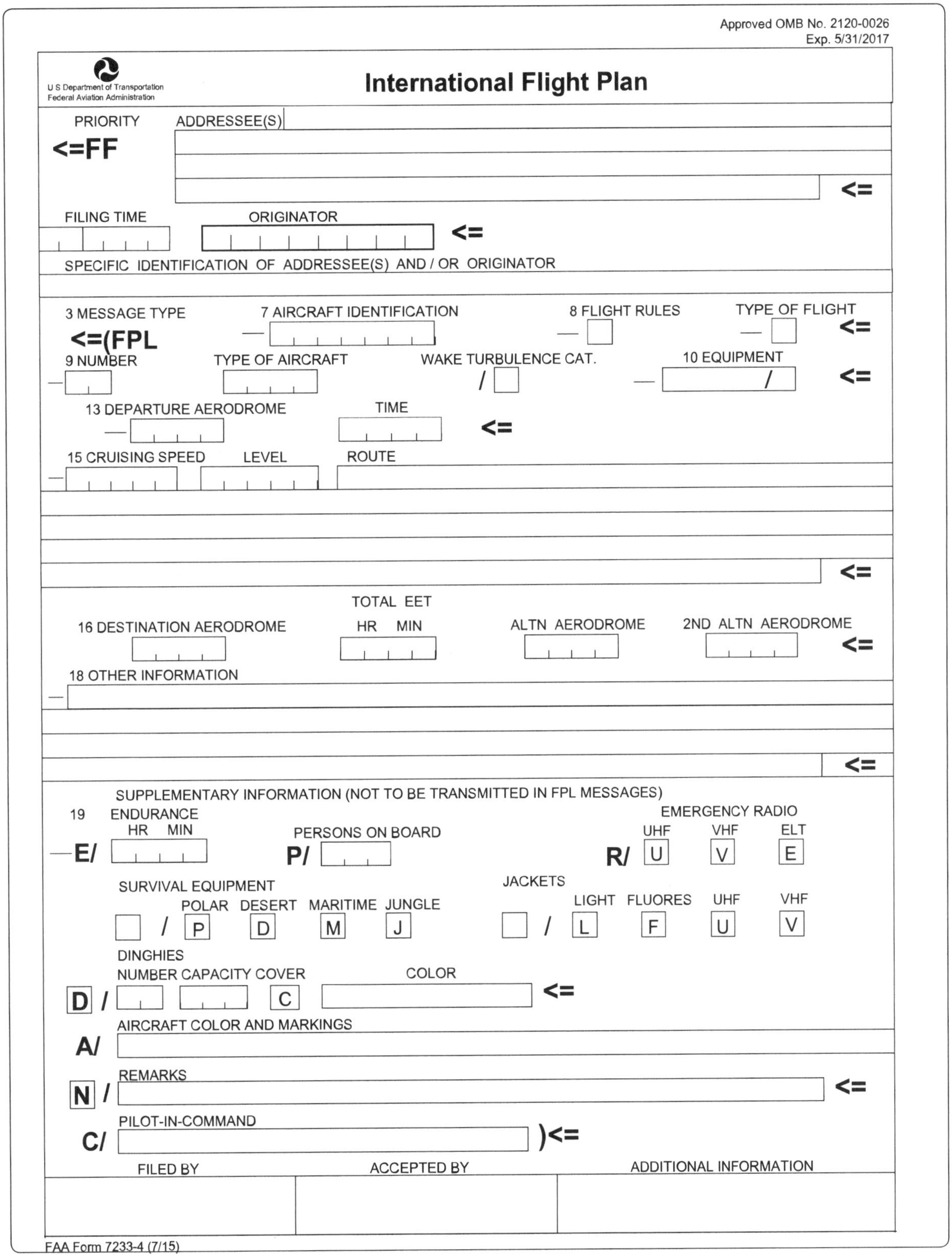
Approved OMB No. 2120-0026
Exp. 5/31/2017

U S Department of Transportation
Federal Aviation Administration

International Flight Plan

PRIORITY <=FF
ADDRESSEE(S) <=

FILING TIME
ORIGINATOR <=

SPECIFIC IDENTIFICATION OF ADDRESSEE(S) AND / OR ORIGINATOR

3 MESSAGE TYPE <=(FPL
7 AIRCRAFT IDENTIFICATION
8 FLIGHT RULES
TYPE OF FLIGHT <=

9 NUMBER
TYPE OF AIRCRAFT
WAKE TURBULENCE CAT. /
10 EQUIPMENT / <=

13 DEPARTURE AERODROME
TIME <=

15 CRUISING SPEED
LEVEL
ROUTE <=

16 DESTINATION AERODROME
TOTAL EET HR MIN
ALTN AERODROME
2ND ALTN AERODROME <=

18 OTHER INFORMATION <=

SUPPLEMENTARY INFORMATION (NOT TO BE TRANSMITTED IN FPL MESSAGES)
19 ENDURANCE HR MIN
—E/
PERSONS ON BOARD P/
EMERGENCY RADIO UHF VHF ELT
R/ U V E

SURVIVAL EQUIPMENT
POLAR DESERT MARITIME JUNGLE
/ P D M J
JACKETS
LIGHT FLUORES UHF VHF
/ L F U V

DINGHIES
NUMBER CAPACITY COVER COLOR
D / C <=

AIRCRAFT COLOR AND MARKINGS
A/

REMARKS
N / <=

PILOT-IN-COMMAND
C/)<=

FILED BY
ACCEPTED BY
ADDITIONAL INFORMATION

FAA Form 7233-4 (7/15)

Figure 1A. – Flight Plan Form (not in supplement).

VALID 1600Z FOR USE 0900-1500Z. TEMPS NEG ABV 24000								
FT	3000	6000	9000	12000	18000	24000	30000	34000	39000
EMI	2807	2715-07	2728-10	2842-13	2867-21	2891-30	751041	771150	780855
ALB	0210	9900-07	2714-09	2728-12	2656-19	2777-28	781842	760150	269658
PSB		1509+04	2119+01	2233-04	2262-14	2368-26	781939	760850	780456
STL	2308	2613+02	2422-03	2431-08	2446-19	2461-30	760142	782650	760559

Figure 2. – Winds and Temperatures Aloft Forecast.

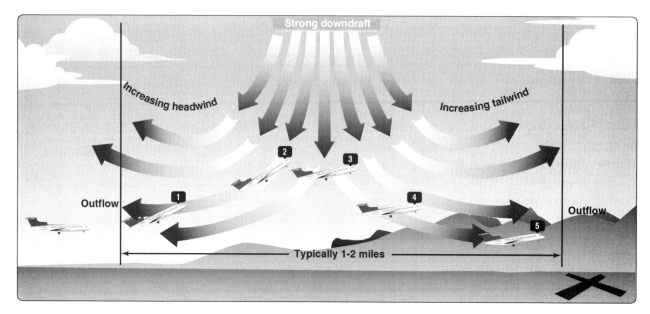

Figure 13. – Microburst Section Chart.

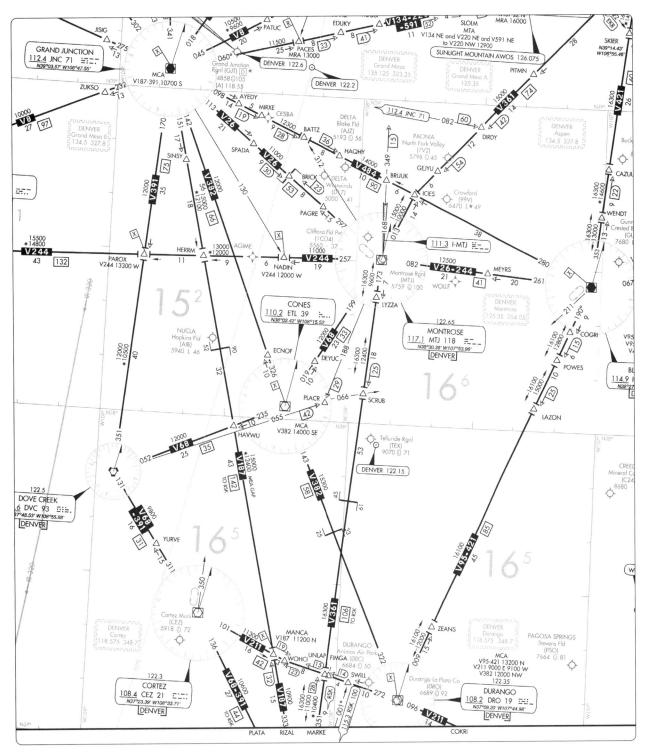

Figure 24. – En Route Low-Altitude Chart Segment.
NOTE: Chart is not to scale and should not be used for navigation. Chart is for testing purposes only.

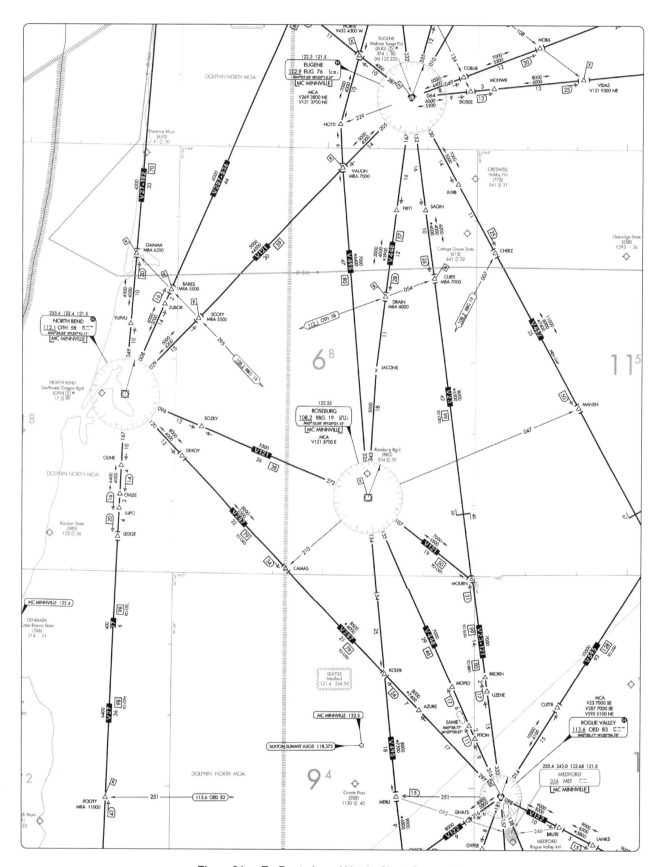

Figure 31. – En Route Low-Altitude Chart Segment.
NOTE: Chart is not to scale and should not be used for navigation. Chart is for testing purposes only.

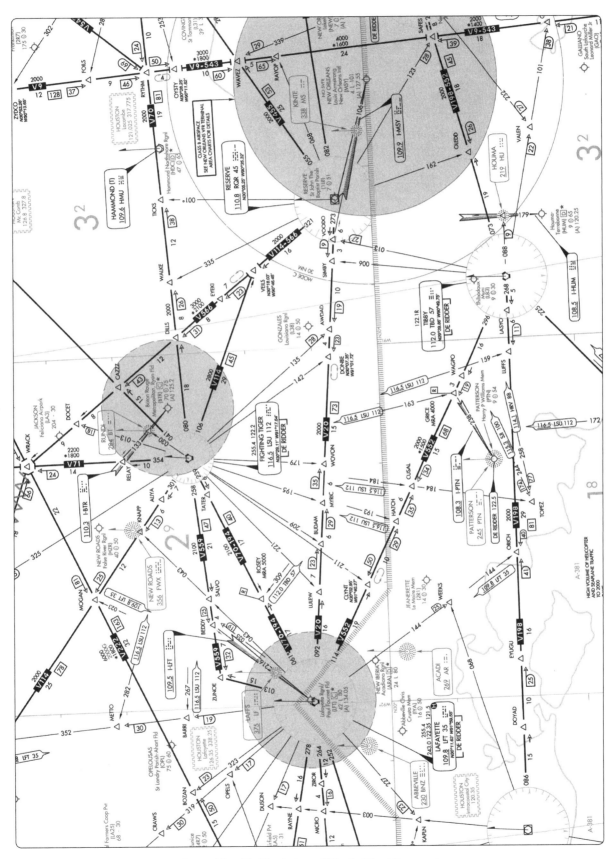

Figure 65. – En Route Low-Altitude Chart Segment.
NOTE: Chart is not to scale and should not be used for navigation. Chart is for testing purposes only.

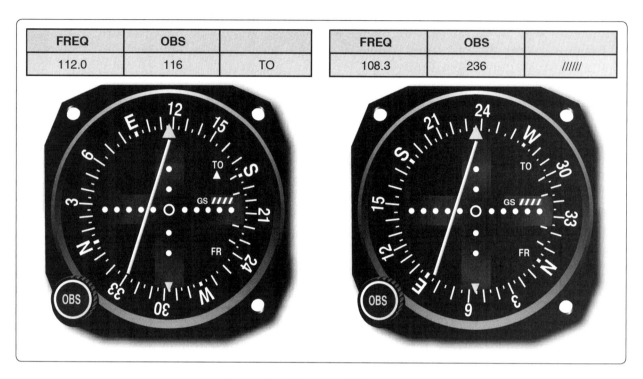

Figure 66. – CDI and OBS Indicators.

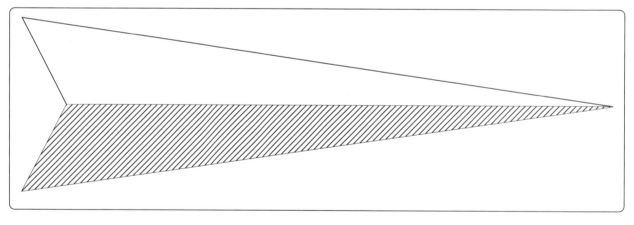

Figure 67. – Localizer Symbol.

Figure 82. – Dual VOR System, Accuracy Check.

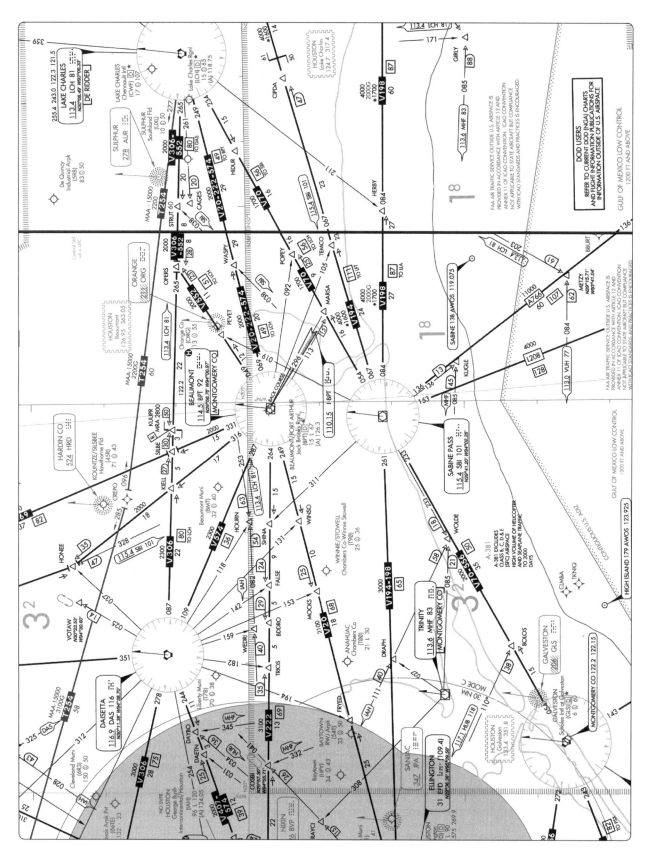

Figure 87. – En Route Low-Altitude Chart Segment.

NOTE: Chart is not to scale and should not be used for navigation. Chart is for testing purposes only.

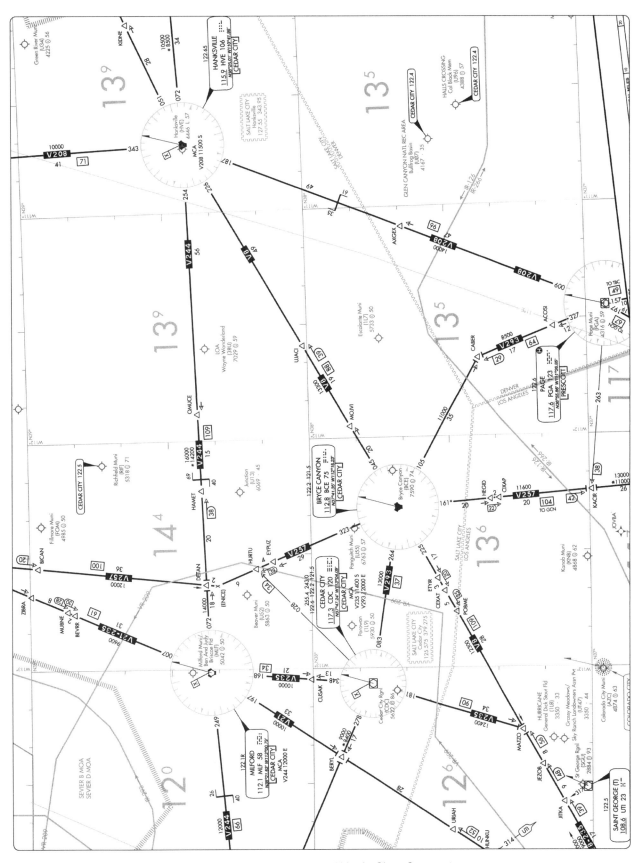

Figure 89. – En Route Low-Altitude Chart Segment.

NOTE: Chart is not to scale and should not be used for navigation. Chart is for testing purposes only.

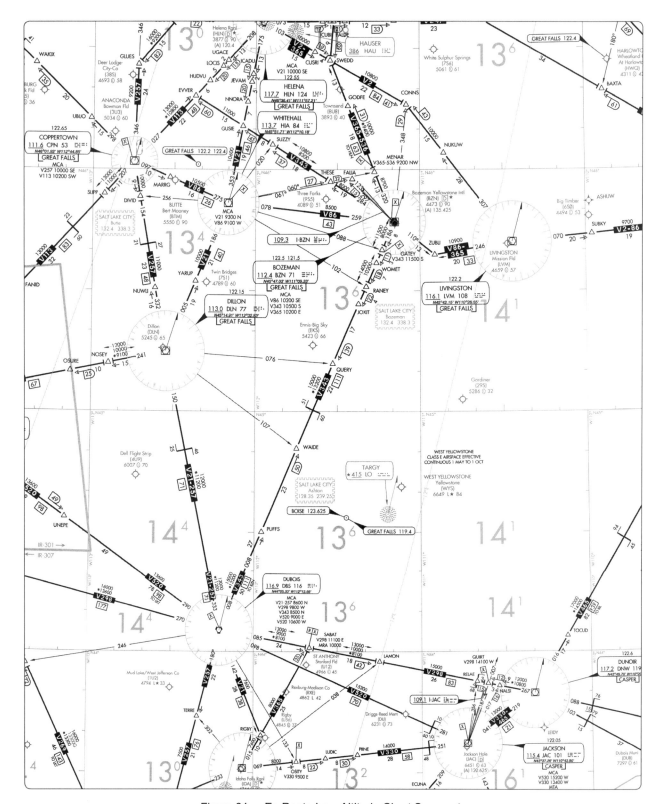

Figure 91. – En Route Low-Altitude Chart Segment.
NOTE: Chart is not to scale and should not be used for navigation. Chart is for testing purposes only.

FREQ	N.M.	KNOTS	MIN
115.0	60	180	20.0

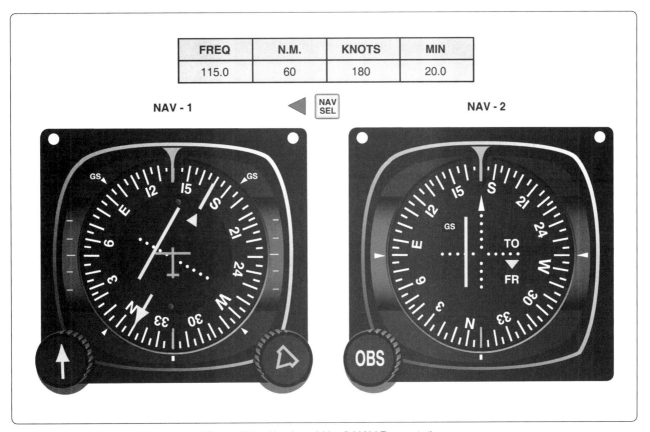

Figure 95. – No. 1 and No. 2 NAV Presentation.

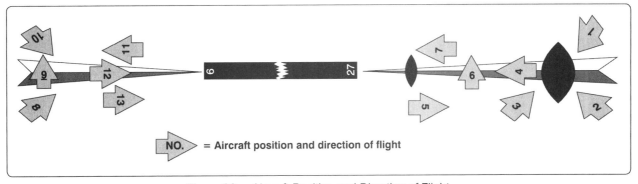

Figure 96. – Aircraft Position and Direction of Flight.

Figure 97. – HSI Presentation.

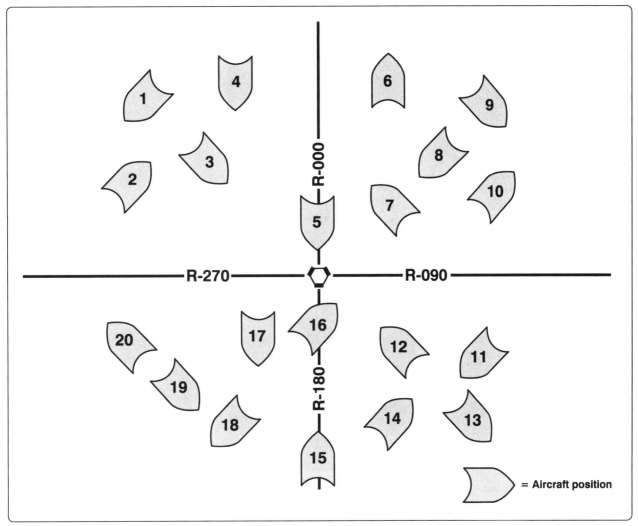

Figure 98. – Aircraft Position.

Figure 99. – HSI Presentation.

Figure 109. – CDI Direction from VORTAC.

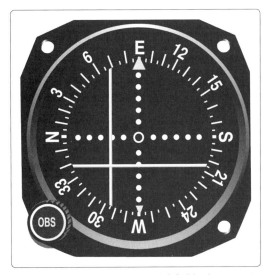

Figure 140. – OBS, ILS, and GS Displacement.

Figure 141. – OBS, ILS, and GS Displacement.

Figure 142. – OBS, ILS, and GS Displacement.

Figure 147. – Instrument Sequence (Unusual Attitude).

OREGON 129

MEDFORD

ROGUE VALLEY INTL – MEDFORD (MFR)   3 N   UTC–8(–7DT)   N42°22.45′ W122°52.41′   **KLAMATH FALLS**
  1335   B   S4   **FUEL** 100LL, JET A   OX 1, 3   TPA—See Remarks   Class I, ARFF Index B   **H–3B, L–2I**
  NOTAM FILE MFR   **IAP, AD**
  RWY 14–32: H8800X150 (ASPH–GRVD)   S–200, D–200, 2S–175,
    2D–400   HIRL   CL
    RWY 14: MALSR. TDZL. PAPI(P4L)—GA 3.0° TCH 73′. 0.4% up.
    RWY 32: REIL. PAPI(P4R)—GA 3.0° TCH 50′. 0.5% down.
  RUNWAY DECLARED DISTANCE INFORMATION
    RWY 14: TORA–8800   TODA–8800   ASDA–8800   LDA–8800
    RWY 32: TORA–8800   TODA–8800   ASDA–8800   LDA–8800
  AIRPORT REMARKS: Attended 1300–0800Z‡. For fuel after hrs call
    541–779–5451, or 541–842–2254. Bird haz large flocks of
    migratory waterfowl in vicinity Nov–May. Terminal apron clsd to acft
    exc scheduled air carrier and flts with prior permission. PPR for
    unscheduled ops with more than 30 passenger seats, call arpt ops
    541–776–7228. Tran tie–downs avbl thru FBOs only. Rwy 32
    preferred for tkfs and ldgs when twr clsd. TPA—2304(969) for
    propeller acft, 2804(1469) for turbo acft. PAPI Rwy 14 and VASI
    Rwy 32 on continuously. ACTIVATE HIRL Rwy 14–32, MALSR Rwy
    14, REIL Rwy 32, TDZL Rwy 14, centerline lgts Rwy 14 and Rwy
    32, and twy lgts—CTAF. Ldg fee applies to all corporate acft and all
    other acft with weight exceeding 12,500 lbs.
  WEATHER DATA SOURCES: ASOS (541) 776–1238 SAWRS.
  COMMUNICATIONS: CTAF 119.4   ATIS 127.25   UNICOM 122.95
    MEDFORD RCO 122.65 (MC MINNVILLE RADIO)
  ℞ **CASCADE APP/DEP CON** 124.3 (1400–0730Z‡)
    SEATTLE CENTER APP/DEP CON 124.85 (0730–1400Z‡)
    TOWER 119.4 (1400–0500Z‡) **GND CON** 121.8
  AIRSPACE: CLASS D svc 1400–0500Z‡ other times CLASS E.
  VOR TEST FACILITY (VOT) 117.2
  RADIO AIDS TO NAVIGATION: NOTAM FILE MFR.
    (H) VORTACW 113.6   OED   Chan 83   N42°28.77′ W122°54.78′   145° 6.6 NM to fld. 2083/19E.   **HIWAS.**
    VOR portion unusable:
      260°–270° byd 35 NM blo 9,000′
      290°–300° byd 35 NM blo 8,500′
    MEDFORD NDB (MHW) 356   MEF   N42°23.50′ W122°52.73′   151° 1.1 NM to fld.
    NDB unusable:
      220°–240° byd 15 NM
    PUMIE NDB (LOM) 373   MF   N42°27.06′ W122°54.80′ 143° 4.9 NM to fld. LOM unusable 260°–270° beyond 10 NM.
      Unmonitored when ATCT closed.
    ILS/DME 110.3   I–MFR   Chan 40   Rwy 14.   Class IA.   LOM PUMIE NDB. LOM unusable 260°–270° beyond 10 NM.
      Unmonitored when ATCT closed. Localizer backcourse unusable byd 11 NM blo 7,000′, byd 13 NM blo 8,300′, byd
      17 NM blo 8,700′. Localizer backcourse unusable byd 20° left of course.

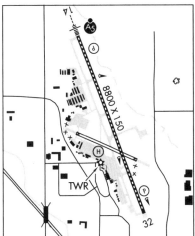

MEMALOOSE (See IMNAHA on page 122)

MILLER MEM AIRPARK (See VALE on page 145)

MONUMENT MUNI (12S)   1 NW   UTC–8(–7DT)   N44°49.89′ W119°25.78′   **SEATTLE**
  2323   TPA—3323(1000)   NOTAM FILE MMV
  RWY 14–32: H2104X29 (ASPH)
    RWY 14: Hill.
  AIRPORT REMARKS: Unattended. Intermittently clsd winters due to snow. Wildlife on and invof arpt. Rwy ends marked at each
    corner by a single white tire.
  COMMUNICATIONS: CTAF 122.9

MULINO STATE (See PORTLAND–MULINO on page 137)

Figure 165. – Excerpt from Chart Supplement.

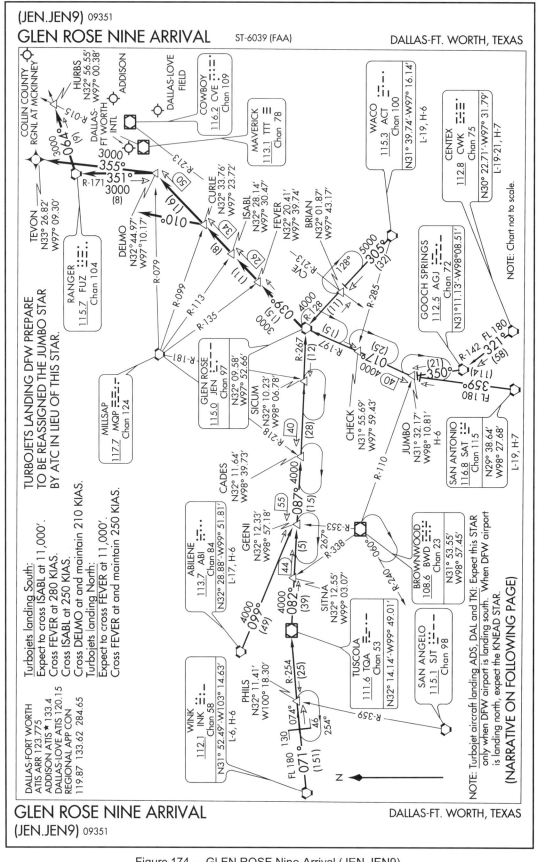

Figure 174. – GLEN ROSE Nine Arrival (JEN.JEN9).

(JEN.JEN9) 09351
GLEN ROSE NINE ARRIVAL   ST-6039 (FAA)   DALLAS-FT. WORTH, TEXAS

ARRIVAL DESCRIPTION

ABILENE TRANSITION (ABI.JEN9): From over ABI VORTAC via R-099 to GEENI INT, then via JEN R-267 to JEN VORTAC. Thence. . . .
CENTEX TRANSITION (CWK.JEN9): From over CWK VORTAC via CWK R-321 and AGJ R-142 to AGJ VORTAC, then via AGJ R-350 to JUMBO INT, then via JEN R-197 to JEN VORTAC. Thence . . . .
JUMBO TRANSITION (JUMBO.JEN9): From over JUMBO INT via JEN R-197 to JEN VORTAC. Thence . . . .
SAN ANTONIO TRANSITION (SAT.JEN9): From over SAT VORTAC via SAT R-359 to JUMBO INT, then via JEN R-197 to JEN VORTAC. Thence . . . .
WACO TRANSITION (ACT.JEN9): From over ACT VORTAC via ACT R-305 and JEN R-128 to JEN VORTAC. Thence. . . .
WINK TRANSITION (INK.JEN9): From over INK VORTAC via INK R-071 and TQA R-254 to TQA VOR/DME, then via TQA R-082 to GEENI INT, then via JEN R-267 to JEN VORTAC. Thence. . . .

. . . . ALL AIRCRAFT: From over JEN VORTAC via JEN R-039, thence . . . .

ALL AIRCRAFT LANDING NORTH: To CURLE INT, expect vectors to final approach course.

JETS LANDING SOUTH: To DELMO, depart DELMO heading 355°.
For /E, /F, /G and /R (RNP 2.0) EQUIPMENT SUFFIXED AIRCRAFT: From over DELMO WP direct TEVON WP, expect vector to final approach course prior to TEVON WP. If not received by TEVON fly present heading.
NON TURBOJETS LANDING SOUTH: To CURLE INT, depart CURLE heading 010° for vectors to final approach course.

AIRCRAFT LANDING DAL, ADS, TKI: To DELMO INT, depart DELMO via FUZ R-171 to FUZ VORTAC then FUZ R-064 to HURBS INT, expect vectors to final approach course.

GLEN ROSE NINE ARRIVAL   DALLAS-FT. WORTH, TEXAS
(JEN.JEN9) 09351

Figure 175. – GLEN ROSE Nine Arrival (JEN.JEN9).

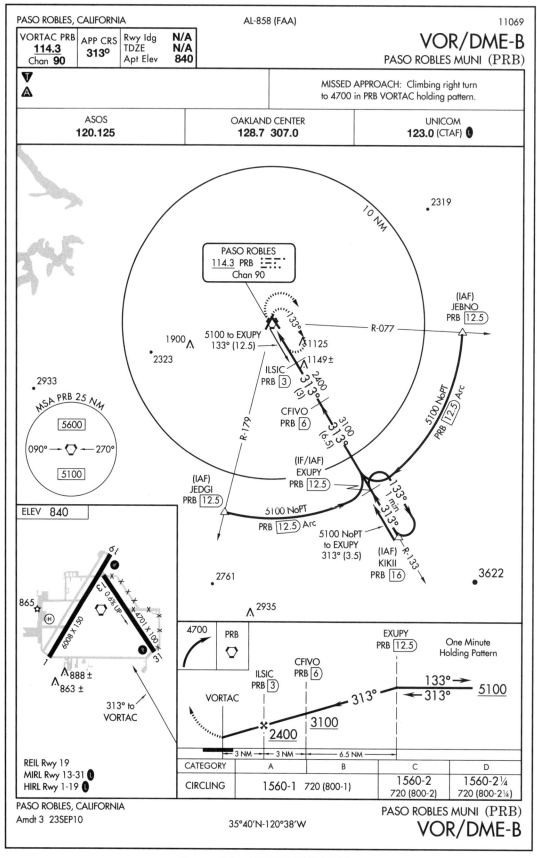

Figure 192. – VOR/DME-B (PRB).

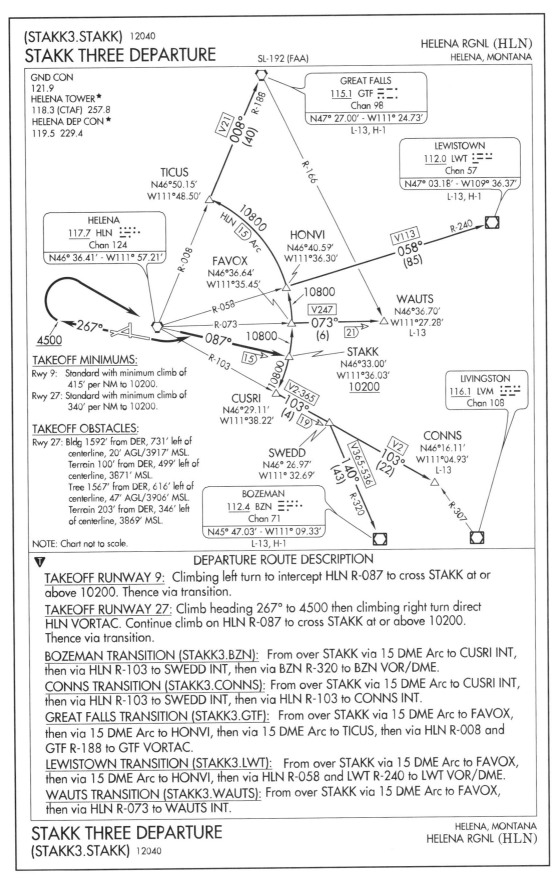

STAKK THREE DEPARTURE
(STAKK3.STAKK) 12040

HELENA, MONTANA
HELENA RGNL (HLN)

Figure 211. – STAKK Three Departure (STAKK3.STAKK) (HLN).

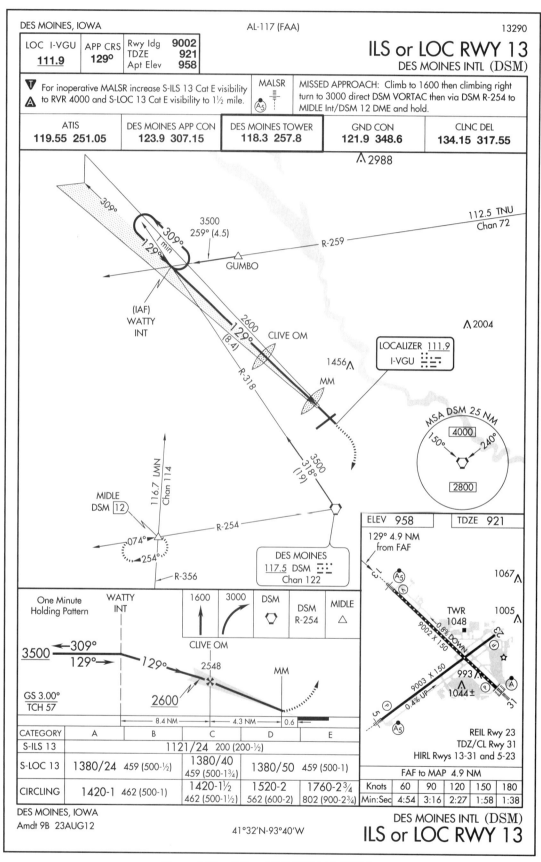

Figure 217. – ILS or LOC RWY 13 (DSM).

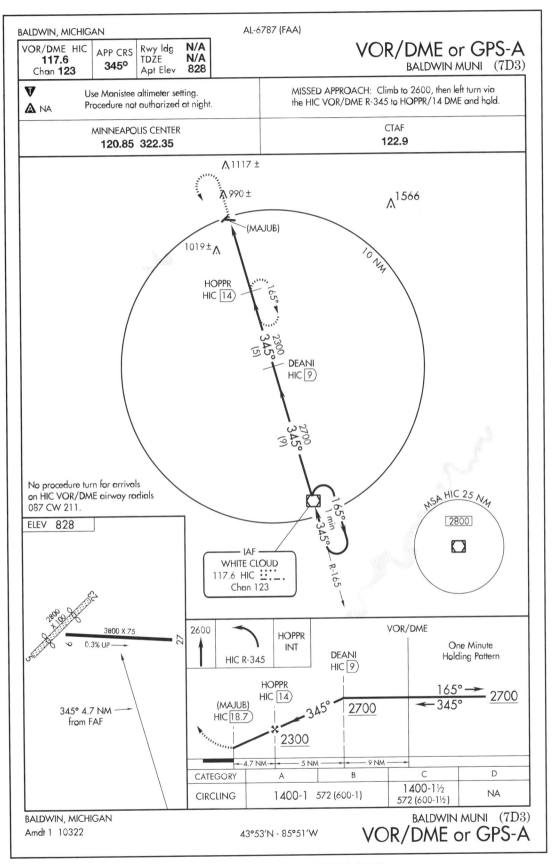

Figure 230. – VOR/DME or GPS-A (7D3).

130	MICHIGAN	

BALDWIN MUNI (7D3)   2 S   UTC–5(–4DT)   N43°52.53´ W85°50.53´   CHICAGO
828   TPA—1828(1000)   NOTAM FILE LAN   L–281
RWY 09–27: H3800X75 (ASPH)   S–10   0.3% up E   IAP
  RWY 09: Trees.
  RWY 27: Trees.
RWY 05–23: 2800X100 (TURF)
  RWY 05: Thld dsplcd 800´. Trees.
  RWY 23: Thld dsplcd 800´. Trees.
AIRPORT REMARKS: Unattended. Deer on and invof arpt. Arpt CLOSED Nov
  thru Apr; no snow removal. Arpt manager cell 231–250–2551. Rwy
  09–27 sfc considerable pavement cracking with vegetation growing
  through cracks. Rwy 05–23 and dsplcd thlds marked with 3´ yellow
  cones.
COMMUNICATIONS: CTAF 122.9
Ⓡ MINNEAPOLIS CENTER APP/DEP CON 120.85
RADIO AIDS TO NAVIGATION: NOTAM FILE LAN.
  WHITE CLOUD (L) VOR/DME 117.6   HIC   Chan 123   N43°34.49´
    W85°42.97´   344° 18.9 NM to fld. 920/1W.
  VOR/DME unusable:
    020°–090° byd 30 NM blo 3,000´
  DME portion unusable:
    270°–290° byd 35 NM blo 3,000´

BANGU   N45°00.88´ W84°48.49´   NOTAM FILE GLR.   LAKE HURON
NDB (LOM) 375   GL   097° 4.5 NM to Gaylord Rgnl. Unmonitored.

BANNISTER

SHADY LAWN FLD (4M4)   2 E   UTC–5(–4DT)   N43°07.72´ W84°22.88´   CHICAGO
680   TPA—1680(1000)   NOTAM FILE LAN
RWY 09–27: 1850X50 (TURF)   LIRL
  RWY 09: Bldg.
  RWY 27: Trees.
AIRPORT REMARKS: Attended irregularly. Ultralight and AG activity on and invof arpt. Deer and birds on and invof arpt. Crops
  adjacent to rwy during summer months. NSTD LIRL color and configuration, by prior arrangement. Rwy 09 and Rwy 27
  marked by 3´ yellow cones.
COMMUNICATIONS: CTAF 122.9

BARAGA (2P4)   4 W   UTC–5(–4DT)   N46°47.10´ W88°34.67´   GREEN BAY
845   TPA—1845(1000)   NOTAM FILE GRB
RWY 09–27: 2200X100 (TURF)
  RWY 09: Trees.
  RWY 27: Trees.
AIRPORT REMARKS: Unattended. Arpt CLOSED Nov–Apr except to ski equipped acft. 25´ p–line 850´ from thld Rwy 27. Deer
  and birds on and invof arpt.
COMMUNICATIONS: CTAF 122.9

BATH

UNIVERSITY AIRPARK (41G)   2 NW   UTC–5(–4DT)   N42°50.42´ W84°28.75´   DETROIT
856   B   S2   NOTAM FILE LAN
RWY 08–26: 1988X100 (TURF)   LIRL
  RWY 08: Trees.
  RWY 26: Tree.
AIRPORT REMARKS: Attended irregularly. Rwy 08–26 occasionally soft/wet areas E end during spring thaw and after heavy rain.
  ACTIVATE LIRL Rwy 08–26 and NSTD rotating bcn—122.85. NSTD flashing strobe and alternating white/red bcn. Rwy
  08–26 marked with 3´ yellow cones.
COMMUNICATIONS: CTAF 122.9

BATOL   N42°21.72´ W85°11.07´   NOTAM FILE BTL.   CHICAGO
NDB (MHW/LOM) 272   BT   225° 4.4 NM to W K Kellogg.   L–281

Figure 231. – Excerpt from Chart Supplement.

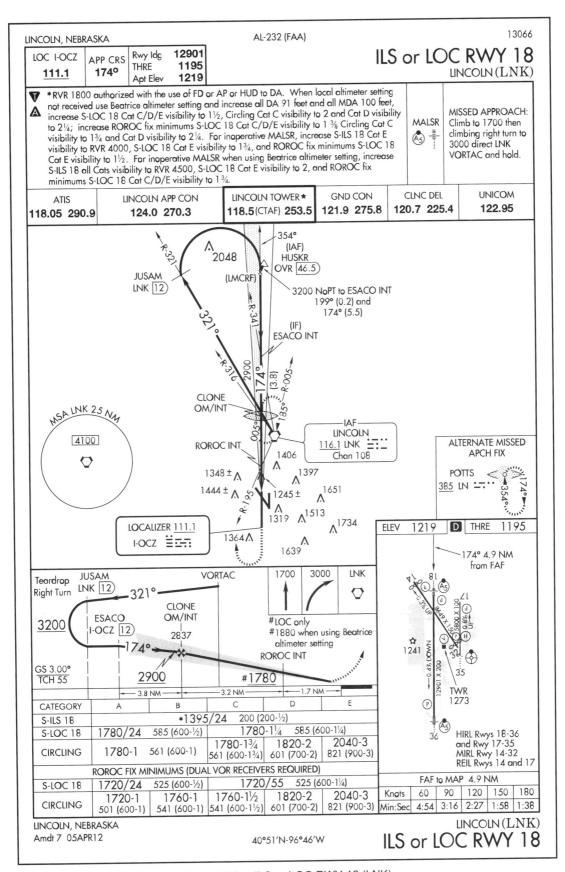

Figure 234. – ILS or LOC RWY 18 (LNK).

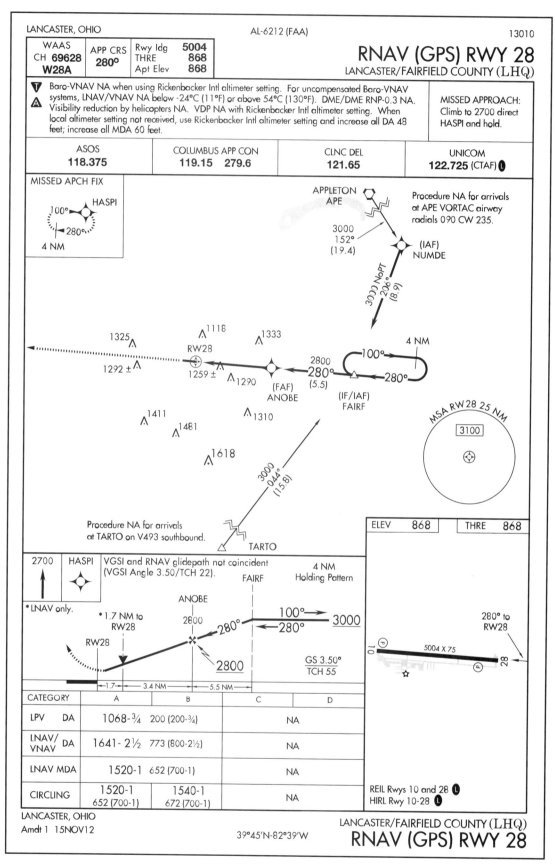

Figure 238. – RNAV (GPS) RWY 28 (LHQ).

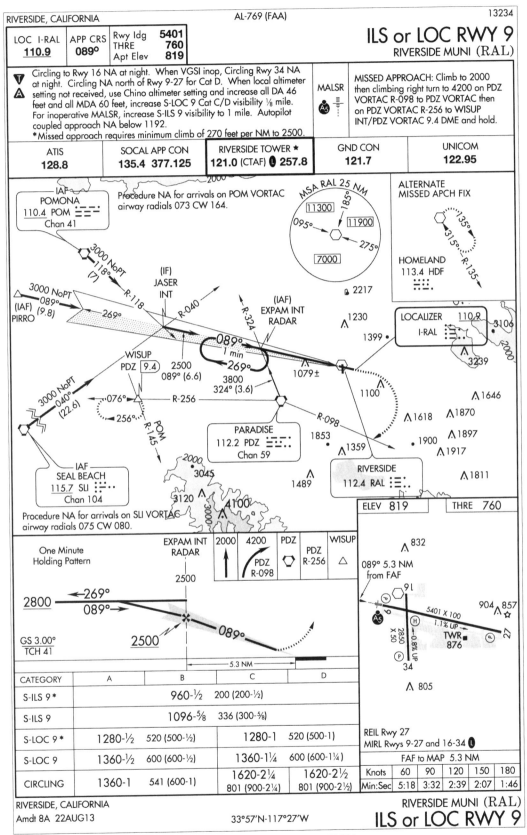

Figure 247. – ILS or RWY 9 (RAL).

APPENDIX B:
USE OF A FLIGHT SIMULATION TRAINING DEVICE OR AN AVIATION TRAINING DEVICE

A flight simulation training device or aviation training device can be an extremely important teaching tool in your instrument training. It can be used to teach the instrument scan, visualization of position, holding, and the approach procedures far more efficiently and cost-effectively than an airplane. These devices can be stopped in mid-flight to allow discussion of problems and can be reset so that difficult portions of a procedure can be practiced repeatedly. Training received in a flight simulation training device or an aviation training device must be logged with an authorized instructor.

Definitions

1. **Flight simulation training devices (FSTD)** are full flight simulators (FFS) or flight training devices (FTD).

    a. **Full flight simulator (FFS)** means a device that

        1) Is a full-size cockpit replica of a specific type of aircraft, or make, model, and series of aircraft

        2) Includes the hardware and software necessary to represent the aircraft in ground and flight operations

        3) Uses a force cueing system that provides cues at least equivalent to those cues provided by a 3° freedom-of-motion system

        4) Uses a visual system that provides at least a 45° horizontal field of view and a 30° vertical field of view simultaneously for each pilot

        5) Has been evaluated, qualified, and approved by the FAA in accordance with 14 CFR 61.4(a)

        6) Includes FFS levels A through D

    b. **Flight training device (FTD)** means a device that

        1) Is a full-size replica of the instruments, equipment panels, and controls of an aircraft in an open flight deck area or in an enclosed cockpit, including the hardware and software for the systems installed that are necessary to simulate the aircraft in ground and flight operations

        2) Need not have a force (motion) cueing or visual system

        3) Has been evaluated, qualified, and approved by the FAA, or has been authorized for specific use under 14 CFR 61.4(a) or (b), as appropriate

        4) Includes levels 4 through 7 (for airplane)

2. An **aviation training device (ATD)** is a training device, other than an FFS or FTD, that has been evaluated, qualified, and approved by the Administrator.

    a. This includes a replica of aircraft instruments, equipment, panels, and controls in an open flight deck area or an enclosed aircraft cockpit.

    b. It includes the hardware and software necessary to represent a category and class of aircraft (or set of aircraft) operations in ground and flight conditions having the appropriate range of capabilities and systems installed in the device for the specific **Basic** or **Advanced** qualification level.

    c. ATDs cannot be used for practical tests, aircraft type specific training, or for an aircraft type rating.

d. **A basic aviation training device (BATD) is a device that**

1) Meets minimum acceptable criteria of AC 61-136B, Appendix B, BATD

2) Provides an adequate training platform and design for both procedural and operational performance tasks specific to the ground and flight training requirements for Private Pilot Certificate and instrument rating per 14 CFR Parts 61 and 141

3) Provides an adequate platform for both procedural and operational performance tasks required for instrument experience and pilot time

4) The FAA finds acceptable in a manner described in AC 61-136B

e. **An advanced aviation training device (AATD) is a device that**

1) Meets or exceeds the criteria outlined in AC 61-136B, Appendix B, BATD

2) Meets or exceeds the criteria outlined in AC 61-136B, Appendix C, AATD

3) Provides an adequate training platform for both procedural and operational performance tasks specific to the ground and flight training requirements for Private Pilot Certificate, instrument rating, Commercial Pilot Certificate, Airline Transport Pilot (ATP) Certificate, and Flight Instructor Certificate per Parts 61 and 141

4) Provides an adequate platform and design for both procedural and operational performance tasks required for instrument experience, the instrument proficiency check, and pilot time

5) The FAA finds acceptable in a manner described in AC 61-136B

NOTE: An AATD, however, may be used for some of the required tasks of an instrument proficiency check (IPC).

ATD Approval for Part 61

1. To be approved for use for pilot training and experience requirements under Part 61, an ATD should

   a. Be capable of providing procedural training in all areas of operation for which it is to be used

      1) Those tasks should be specified in an acceptable training curriculum or as authorized by the FAA and meet the description and suggested criteria outlined in AC 61-136B, Appendix D.

   b. Have the Letter of Authorization (LOA), Qualification and Approval Guide (QAG), and performance information for the aircraft configurations being represented

2. For more detailed information about ATDs, refer to FAA AC 61-136B, *FAA Approval of Aviation Training Devices and Their Use for Training and Experience.*

ATD Approval for Part 141

1. Notwithstanding Part 61 criteria, the local Flight Standards office may approve an ATD as part of an overall Part 141 school curriculum approval and certification process.

Part 141 – Appendix C Instrument Rating Course

1. Instrument training in a simulator may be credited as follows:

   a. FFS: Up to 50% of the required course hours can be logged.

   b. FTD: Up to 40% of the required course hours can be logged.

   c. AATD: Up to 40% of the required course hours can be logged.

   d. BATD: Up to 25% of the required course hours can be logged.

   e. Combination ATD and FTD: Up to 40% of the required course hours can be logged (notwithstanding BATD 25% limit).

   f. Combination FFS, FTD, and ATD: Up to 50% of the required course hours can be logged (notwithstanding the FTD 40%, AATD 40%, and BATD 25% limits).

      1) The device must be approved and authorized by the FAA.

      2) The FAA must approve the instrument training and instrument tasks performed in the device.

      3) An authorized instructor must provide the instrument time in the device.

      4) The ATD must be used in conjunction with an FAA-approved integrated ground and flight instrument training syllabus.

Part 61 – Instrument Rating Course

1. BATD: maximum of 10 hours
2. AATD: maximum of 20 hours
3. Combination FFS, FTD, ATD: maximum of 20 hours

   a. The device must be approved and authorized by the FAA.

   b. The FAA must approve the instrument training and instrument tasks performed in the device.

   c. An authorized instructor must provide the instrument time in the device.

ENROLLMENT CERTIFICATE

This is to certify that

_____

is enrolled in the

Federal Aviation Administration

approved Instrument Rating Course

conducted by

_____
(name of school and certificate number)

_____
Chief Instructor

_____
Date of Enrollment

Gleim Publications, Inc.
PO Box 12848
Gainesville, Florida 32604
(800) 874-5346
(352) 375-0772
(352) 375-6940 FAX
GleimAviation.com
aviationteam@gleim.com

GLEIM®
Aviation

GRADUATION CERTIFICATE ✈

This is to certify that

_____

has satisfactorily completed all stages, tests, and
course requirements and has graduated from the
FEDERAL AVIATION ADMINISTRATION
approved Instrument Rating Course

conducted by _____
(name of school and certificate number)

The graduate has received _____ hours of cross-country training.

_____
Chief Instructor

_____
Date of Graduation

GLEIM®

Aviation

Gleim Publications, Inc.
PO Box 12848
Gainesville, Florida 32604
(800) 874-5346
(352) 375-0772
(352) 375-6940 FAX
GleimAviation.com
aviationteam@gleim.com